THE CAMBRIDGE ANCIENT HISTORY

EDITORS

Volumes I–VI	*Volumes* VII, VIII
J. B. BURY, M.A., F.B.A.	S. A. COOK, LITT.D.
S. A. COOK, LITT.D.	F. E. ADCOCK, M.A.
F. E. ADCOCK, M.A.	M. P. CHARLESWORTH, M.A.

THIRD VOLUME OF PLATES

Cambridge University Press
Fetter Lane, London

New York
Bombay, Calcutta, Madras
Toronto
Macmillan

Tokyo
Maruzen Company, Ltd

THE
CAMBRIDGE
ANCIENT HISTORY

EDITED BY

S. A. COOK, Litt. D.

F. E. ADCOCK, M. A.

M. P. CHARLESWORTH, M. A.

VOLUME OF PLATES III

PREPARED BY

C. T. SELTMAN, M. A.

CAMBRIDGE

AT THE UNIVERSITY PRESS

1930

31973

PRINTED IN GREAT BRITAIN

PREFACE

The illustrations collected in this volume contrast in many respects with those of its predecessor. The latter was devoted almost entirely to Greek art; here will be found objects ranging from Britain to India, from Spain to Central Asia. This altered aspect is due to the fact that the volume provides illustrations for volumes vii and viii of the *Cambridge Ancient History*, which are concerned with that greatly extended horizon of which men became aware through the conquests of Alexander and the westward expansion of Rome. Yet the Mediterranean holds the centre of interest; hence the products of the Hellenistic Age, sculpture, painting, architecture and the minor arts, occupy the chief place. But, in addition to the plates illustrating such subjects, there will be found illustrations of Celtic, Iberian, Thracian, Bosporan and Carthaginian products, and of numerous coins which have been mentioned in the text of the *History*. If Italy and Rome appear to have received scant notice this is because the discussion of their art is reserved for volume ix and for the plates which will illustrate it.

For the selection of the subjects illustrated and for the commentaries on them the volume is indebted to the writers of the several chapters concerned. Mr de Navarro has dealt with the Celtic products, Professor Schulten with the Iberian, Professor Kazarow with the art of the Thracians. Professor Rostovtzeff has described the plates illustrating his chapters on the Bosporan kingdom, Pergamum, Rhodes, Delos and Hellenistic commerce. The commentary on Hellenistic sculpture, painting and architecture is the work of Professor Ashmole; Mr Charlesworth has selected the illustrations of Carthaginian handicraft. For the descriptions of the coins the compiler of the volume is responsible.

The main purpose of this book will be achieved if it proves helpful to readers of volumes vii and viii. Yet it may have an interest of its own. The first volume of plates, it was suggested, might indicate many of the influences which contributed to the formation of Greek art; the second showed the growth of that art to full maturity; the third depicts the civilized world and its barbarian fringes eagerly borrowing, selecting, modifying the artistic ideas of the Greeks.

v

PREFACE

Acknowledgments are gratefully made to Professor Ashmole, Dr A. B. Cook, Professor Ebert, Monsieur Goury, Professor Kazarow, Professor Rostovtzeff and Professor Schulten for the use of photographs in their possession, and to the Directors of the British Museum and of the Austrian Archaeological Institute for permission to reproduce numerous pictures. The Directors of the Museums in Berlin, Cologne, Copenhagen, Munich, Oxford, Paris and Rhodes have either generously supplied photographs or sanctioned the reproduction of antiquities under their care. To Dr G. F. Hill, Keeper of Coins and Medals in the British Museum, to Professor K. Regling and Monsieur J. Babelon of the Cabinets of Coins in Berlin and Paris, as well as to Monsieur R. Jameson and Mr E. T. Newell, thanks are due for the provision of plaster casts and photographs of coins.

Professor Ashmole desires to thank Mr E. S. G. Robinson of the British Museum for selecting the coins illustrating portraiture on p. 164; Mr de Navarro thanks Professor and Mrs Chadwick for assistance on various points. The volume is, in particular, indebted to Professor Rostovtzeff for the use of eight of his pictures of Hellenistic terracottas. Messrs F. Bruckmann of Munich have generously supplied a photograph (p. 178 [b]) which is due to appear in a forthcoming publication (Hermann, *Denkmäler der Malerei des Altertums*).

Reproduction from the books specified has been sanctioned by the following publishers:

C. A. Beck, Munich (Furtwängler, *Kleine Schriften*).

E. de Boccard, Paris (*Bulletin de Correspondance Hellénique*, 1884).

F. Bruckmann A.G., Munich (Brunn, *Denkmäler*; Pfuhl, *Malerei und Zeichnung der Griechen*; Schulten, *Numantia*).

The Clarendon Press, Oxford (Rostovtzeff, *Iranians and Greeks in South Russia*; ib. *History of the Ancient World*).

W. de Gruyter and Co., Berlin (Ebert, *Reallexikon der Vorgeschichte*; Humann, *Magnesia am Maeander*; Knackfuss, *Das Rathaus von Milet*; Wiegand and Schrader, *Priene*).

Propyläen-Verlag, Berlin (Rodenwaldt, *Die Kunst der Antike, Hellas und Rom*).

Seemann and Co., Leipzig (*Zeitschrift für Bildende Kunst*, 1903).

Société française d'Editions d'Art, Paris (*Pergame*).

PREFACE

The Staff of the University Press again deserve grateful acknowledgment for their accurate care.

Upon the outside cover is a design representing a bronze statuette in Berlin. It is of the third century B.C. and represents a Gallic slinger with a horned helmet and wearing a torque and a belt.

C. T. S.

October 1930

TABLE OF CONTENTS

ix

CONTENTS

x

CONTENTS

xi

CONTENTS

CONTENTS

[a], [b] silver, and [c] bronze coins of the *Achaean League*, 280–146 B.C.
[a] Federal mint; head of Zeus. Rev. monogram **AX** in wreath.
[b] Corinthian mint; types as last, but Pegasus over the monogram.
[c] Argive mint, Zeus Amarios. Rev. **AXAIΩN APΓEIΩN**; Demeter
Panachaia seated. *Brit. Mus. Cat. Peloponnesus*, p. 2, 2, Wt. 2·59 g.;
p. 3, 28, Wt. 2·43 g.; p. 13, 155. (vii, 736.)

[d], [e] Regal coins of cities on the Black Sea after about 290 B.C.
[d] *Sinope*, tetradrachm with Alexander types (cf. *Vol. of Plates*, ii,
8 [n]), in the field **ΣI** and aplustre. *Newell Coll.* [e] *Byzantium*, gold
stater with Lysimachus types (cf. *Vol. of Plates*, ii, 8 [l]); below
Athena a trident. *Naville Catal.* xiii, 676. (vii, 90.)

[f] *Antigonus Gonatas.* Tetradrachm struck to commemorate his
naval victory over the Egyptian fleet off Cos in 258 B.C. Head of
Corinthian Poseidon. Rev. Apollo seated on the prow of the
"Isthmia," the king's flagship, which was dedicated at Delos; on
the prow **BAΣIΛEΩΣ ANTIΓONOY**. Formerly *Pozzi Coll.* Wt.
16·75 g. (vii, 714.)

[g] *Antigonus Gonatas.* Tetradrachm issued after his defeat of the
Gauls at Lysimacheia in 277 B.C. Macedonian shield on which head
of Pan and pedum. Rev. inscription as last; Athena Alkis, in field
Macedonian helmet. Formerly *Pozzi Coll.* Wt. 17 g. (vii, 107, 201.)

[h] *Abdera*, bronze coin. Portrait of Ptolemy III, diademed and
with aegis at neck. Rev. **ABΔHPITΩN**; griffin of Abdera. Struck
probably after 239 B.C. when Ptolemy's general occupied Abdera.
Formerly *Imhoof-Blumer Coll.* (vii, 719.)

[i] *Areus of Sparta*, 310–266 B.C. Tetradrachm with Alexander
types (cf. *Vol. of Plates*, ii, 8 [n]). Rev. inscription **BAΣIΛEOΣ** (*sic*)
APEOΣ. The earliest known Spartan coinage. Lambros, *Peloponnese*,
Pl. IA′, 6. (vii, 99.)

[j] *Cleomenes III of Sparta*, about 228 B.C. Tetradrachm. Portrait
with diadem. Rev. **ΛA**; agalma of helmeted Apollo of Amyclae,
beside him a goat, in field wreath. *B.M.C. Peloponnesus*, p. 121, 1.
Wt. 16·56 g. (vii, 719.)

2

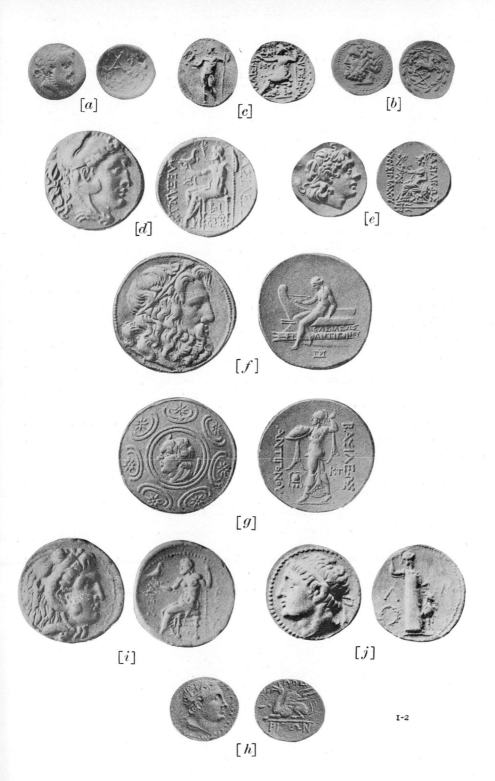

[a]   [c]   [b]

[d]   [e]

[f]

[g]

[i]   [j]

[h]

I-2

COINAGE OF BACTRIA, PERGAMUM, EGYPT AND SYRACUSE

[a], [b] *Bactria and Sogdiana* under *Diodotus*, about 250 B.C. Tetradrachms. A portrait of the same ruler appears on both coins. Rev. Zeus hurling a thunderbolt, eagle before him. [a] **ΒΑΣΙΛΕΩΣ ΑΝΤΙΟΧΟΥ**, [b] **ΒΑΣΙΛΕΩΣ ΔΙΟΔΟΤΟΥ**. *B.M.C. Seleucid Kings*, p. 15, 18. Wt. 16·65 g. *B.M.C. India, Greek and Scythic Kings*, p. 3, 3. Wt. 16·66 g. (vii, 719.)

[c] *Philetaerus*, ruler of *Pergamum* and vassal of the Seleucid House, 284–263 B.C. Tetradrachm. Portrait of Seleucus I. Rev. **ΦΙΛΕΤΑΙ-ΡΟΥ**; Athena seated. *B.M.C. Mysia*, p. 114, 28. Wt. 16·82 g. (vii, 709; viii, 590, 601, 612.)

[d] *Eumenes I*, king of *Pergamum*, 263–241 B.C. Tetradrachm. Portrait of his uncle Philetaerus. Rev. as last coin. *Ibid.* p. 115, 31. Wt. 16·99 g. (vii, 709; viii, 591.)

[e] *Arsinoe II*. Silver tetradrachm. Before 270 B.C. Head of the queen wearing diadem, stephane and veil. Rev. **ΑΡΣΙΝΟΗΣ ΦΙΛΑΔΕΛΦΟΥ**; eagle on thunderbolt. *B.M.C. Ptolemies*, p. 43, 7. Wt. 13·97 g. (vii, 97, 703.)

[f] *Syracuse* under *Agathocles* as *strategos autokrator*, 316–304 B.C. Tetradrachm with old Syracusan types. Head of goddess surrounded by dolphins. Rev. **ΣΥΡΑΚΟΣΙΩΝ**; four-horse chariot, triskeles above. *Bibl. Nat. Paris.* Wt. 17·2 g. (vii, 621.)

[g] *Syracuse* under *Agathocles* as king, 304–289 B.C. Tetradrachm. **ΚΟΡΑΣ**, head of Kore. Rev. **ΑΓΑΘΟΚΛΕΙΟΣ**; Nike erecting trophy, triskeles in field. *Bibl. Nat. Paris.* Wt. 17 g. (vii, 634.)

[a]   [b]

[c]   [d]   [e]

[f]   [g]

Rome, cast bronze libral *as*, about end of fourth century, or first half of third century B.C. Head of bearded Janus. Rev. prow of ship, above, | (sign of value). *Brit. Mus.* The average weight of the Roman libral *as* is 327·45 g. (vii, 433, 607, 608, 662, 663.)

ITALIAN COINAGE

[a], [b] *Rome*, cast bronze libral *semis* and *uncia*, part of the same series as the *as* (p. 6). [a] Head of Jupiter, S (= semis) below. Rev. prow, S above. [b] Head of Bellona. Rev. • under prow. *Brit. Mus.* (vii, 662.)

[c] *Beneventum*, bronze coin struck after 268 B.C. BENEVENTOD, head of Apollo. ΠΡΟΠΟΜ, horse and pentagram. *B.M.C. Italy*, p. 68, 1. (vii, 608.)

[d] Silver didrachm, '*Romano-Campanian*,' having the same types as [c], but on the obv. ROMANO, and on rev. star instead of pentagram. *Brit. Mus.* Wt. 6·84 g. (vii, 608.)

[e] '*Romano-Campanian*' didrachm. Head of Heracles. Rev. ROMANO; she-wolf suckling twins. *Brit. Mus.* Wt. 7·06 g. (vii, 367, 608.)

[f] '*Romano-Campanian*' didrachm. Bearded head in crested Corinthian helmet. Rev. ROMANO; bust of horse, behind ear of corn. The head and ear of corn are Metapontine types; the horse's bust Carthaginian (cf. below, p. 20 [l]). *Brit. Mus.* Wt. 7·45 g. (vii, 608, 649.)

[g], [h], [i] *Roman silver* usually ascribed to 268 B.C. Denarius, quinarius and sestertius with marks of value X, V and HS behind the head of Roma. Rev. ROMA; Castor and Pollux on horseback, stars above them. *Brit. Mus.* Wts. 4·32; 2·24; 1·07 g. (vii, 489, 608, 663.)

[j] *Locri* as ally of *Rome*, about 275 B.C. Didrachm. Head of Zeus resembling that on coins of Pyrrhus. Rev. ΛΟΚΡΩΝ; Locri as ΠΙΣΤΙΣ placing a wreath upon the head of the seated ΡΩΜΑ. *B.M.C. Italy*, p. 365, 15. Wt. 7·08 g. (vii, 654.)

[k] *Rome*, struck bronze *as* reduced to uncial standard after 217 B.C. Types like those of the libral *as* (p. 6), but over the prow SAR, the beginning of the mint-official's name. *Brit. Mus.* (vii, 433; viii, 112.)

8

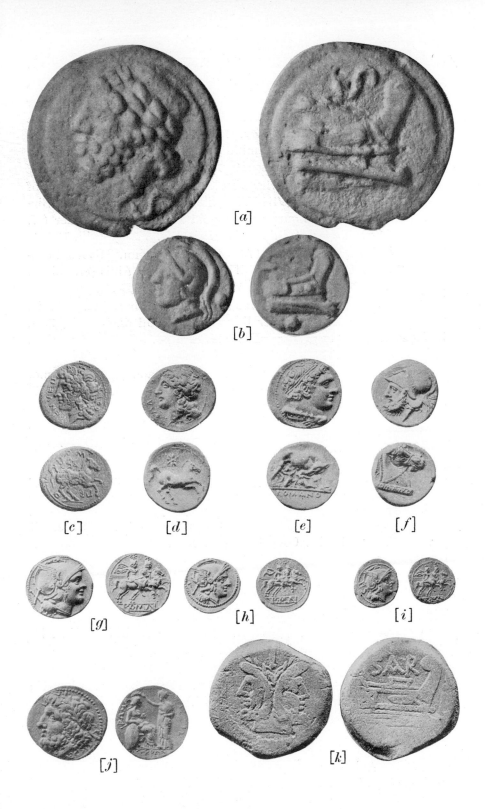

[a]

[b]

[c]   [d]   [e]   [f]

[g]   [h]   [i]

[j]   [k]

COINAGE OF GREECE, ASIA MINOR AND SPAIN

[a] *Roman denarius,* issued about 65 B.C. by a descendant of M. Aemilius Lepidus, to commemorate his legendary guardianship over Ptolemy V in 201 B.C. ALEXSANDREA; head of Tyche of Alexandria wearing turreted crown. Rev. M · LEPIDVS TVTOR REG · ΓΟΝΤΕ · MAX · S · C; M. Aemilius placing a wreath on the head of the boy-king who holds a sceptre. *Brit. Mus.* (viii, 166.)

[b] Gold stater, minted perhaps in Corinth, with the portrait of *Flamininus.* Rev. T · QVINCTI; Nike crowning the name. She resembles closely the figure on the gold staters of Alexander (cf. *Vol. of Plates,* ii, 8 [m], [o]). *Berlin Mus.* Wt. 8·55 g. (viii, 193.)

[c] *Philip V* of Macedon, 220–179 B.C. Tetradrachm. His head diademed. Rev. ΒΑΣΙΛΕΩΣ ΦΙΛΙΠΠΟΥ; Athena Alkis (cf. coin of Antigonus, p. 2 [g]). *Brit. Mus.* Wt. 16·78 g. (viii, 144.)

[d] *Nabis,* king of *Sparta,* 207–192 B.C. Tetradrachm. His portrait, with beard and shaven upper lip, wreathed and diademed. Rev. ΒΑΙΛΕΟΣ (*sic*) ΝΑΒΙΟΣ; Heracles seated. *Brit. Mus.* Wt. 17·04 g. (viii, 189.)

[e] *Orophernes,* pretender to the throne of Cappadocia, 158–157 B.C. Tetradrachm minted in *Priene.* Diademed head. Rev. ΒΑΣΙΛΕΩΣ ΟΡΟΦΕΡΝΟΥ ΝΙΚΗΦΟΡΟΥ; Nike crowning the name (cf. *Vol. of Plates,* ii, 8, [o]); in field, owl on base (mint-mark of Priene). *B.M.C. Galatia, Cappadocia, Syria,* p. 34, 1. Wt. 16·4 g. Found at Priene. (viii, 281.)

[f] *Spanish* silver coin of the weight of a denarius. Iberian legends. Male head. Rev. horseman. *Brit. Mus.* (viii, 309.) The types are derived from [g] below.

[g] Bronze coin of *Hiero II* of *Syracuse,* 274–215 B.C. His portrait diademed. Rev. ΙΕΡΩΝΟΣ; horseman. *Bibl. Nat. Paris.* (viii, 281.)

[h] Bronze coin, 'sextans,' of *Emporium.* Bust of Roma, with two dots as the mark of value on her helmet. Rev. EMPORI; Pegasus. *Naville Catal.* xii. (viii, 281.)

[i] Silver drachma of *Emporium.* Female head and dolphins copied from Syracusan coinage (cf. p. 4 [f]). Rev. ΕΜΓΟΡΙΤΩΝ; Pegasus copied from coins of Corinth (cf. *Vol. of Plates,* ii, 8 [e]). *Jameson Coll.* Wt. 4·56 g. (viii, 311.)

[j] *Gades,* silver coin. Head of Heracles. Rev. Phoenician legend; fish. *Mathey Coll.* Wt. 2·93 g. (viii, 311.)

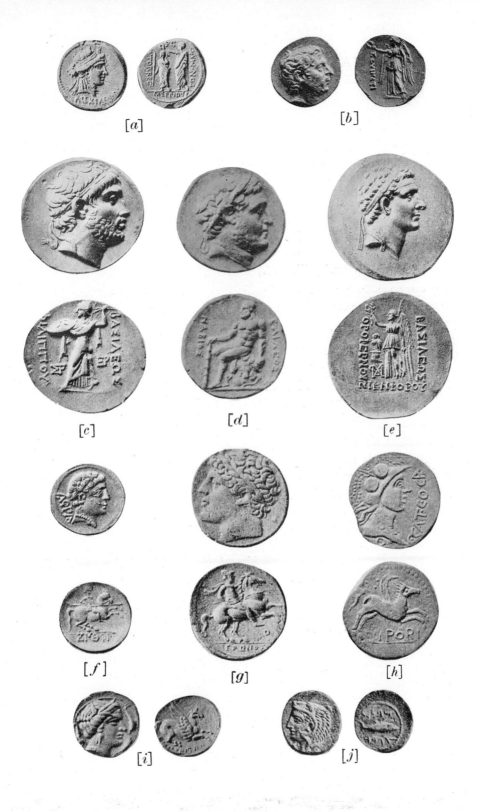

[a]

[b]

[c]

[d]

[e]

[f]

[g]

[h]

[i]

[j]

[a], [b], [c] *Macedon* after division into four *Regiones*, coins issued 158–149 B.C. [a], [b] Tetradrachms of the first and of the second division. Macedonian shield (cf. p. 2 [g]), on which head of Artemis. Rev. club in oak-wreath; **ΜΑΚΕΔΟΝΩΝ ΠΡΩΤΗΣ**, or **ΔΕΥΤΕΡΑΣ**. [c] Bronze coin of the fourth division. Head of Zeus. Rev. as last, but **ΤΕΤΑΡΤΗΣ**. No coins of the third division have been found. [a] *Du Chastel Coll.* [b] *Allatini Coll.* [c] *Berlin Mus.* Wts. 17 g.; 16·75 g. (viii, 277.)

[d] '*Philip*' *Andriscus*, Macedonian Pretender, 149–148 B.C. Tetradrachm. Macedonian shield on which his head in the helmet of the hero Perseus. Rev. types as last coins; **ΒΑΣΙΛΕΩΣ ΦΙΛΙΠΠΟΥ**. Formerly *Pozzi Coll.* Wt. 17·17 g. (viii, 276.)

[e] *Juventius Thalna*, in Macedon. Tetradrachm, 149 B.C. Types as [a] but rev. legend **ΜΑΚΕΔΟΝΩΝ**, **LEG**(atus pro quaestore), above hand holding branch, θαλλός, probably the signet of Thalna. Formerly *Imhoof-Blumer Coll.* Wt. 16·94 g. (viii, 276.)

[f]–[i] Tetradrachms issued by *Antiochus IV Epiphanes*: [f] with the portrait of his nephew, the baby Antiochus; [g] with his own portrait. Both have the same reverse legend and type—'of king Antiochus,' Apollo seated on omphalos, a small tripod in the field, about 175–170 B.C. (viii, 498, 713 *sq.*); [h], [i] about 167 B.C., or later, have on the reverse Zeus Olympios Nikephoros: [h] has a portrait of the king; [i] of the king as Zeus laureate and disguised with a beard. The last bears the long inscription **ΒΑΣΙΛΕΩΣ ΑΝΤΙΟΧΟΥ ΘΕΟΥ ΕΠΙ-ΦΑΝΟΥΣ ΝΙΚΗΦΟΡΟΥ**. (viii, 508.) The heads on all four coins are surrounded by fillet-borders. *B.M.C. Seleucid Kings*, p. 24, 3, Wt. 17·03 g.; p. 34, 4, Wt. 17·02 g.; p. 35, 15, Wt. 16·82 g.; p. 36, 22, Wt. 16·83 g.

COINAGE OF BABYLON, SYRIA, JUDAEA
AND ASIA MINOR

[a] *Timarchus*, satrap of Babylon, as Great King in Babylonia and Media. Tetradrachm, *ca.* 162 B.C. His portrait in Macedonian helmet. Rev. ΒΑΣΙΛΕΩΣ ΜΕΓΑΛΟΥ ΤΙΜΑΡΧΟΥ; the Dioscuri on horseback. The types are copied from those of Eucratides, Great King of Bactria. Formerly *E. F. Weber Coll.* Wt. 15·8 g. (viii, 518.)

[b] *Antiochus VI Dionysus*. Tetradrachm, 145–142 B.C. Head of the boy-king radiate and diademed. Rev. ΒΑΣΙΛΕΩΣ ΑΝΤΙΟΧΟΥ ΕΠΙΦΑΝΟΥΣ ΔΙΟΝΥΣΟΥ; Dioscuri on horseback, in field ΤΡΥ (for Tryphon).

[c] *Tryphon* as *Basileus Autokrator*. Tetradrachm, 142–138 B.C. Diademed head. Rev. ΒΑΣΙΛΕΩΣ ΤΡΥΦΩΝΟΣ ΑΥΤΟΚΡΑ-ΤΟΡΟΣ; Macedonian helmet and ibex-horn. *B.M.C. Seleucid Kings*, p. 63, 3, Wt. 16·53 g.; p. 68, 2, Wt. 15·99 g. (viii, 527.)

[d] The first *Jewish coinage* under *Simon Maccabaeus*. Bronze half-shekel of the year 136/5 B.C. Citron (*ethrog*) between two bundles of twigs (*lulab*), around 'In the fourth year—one-half.' Rev. palm-tree between two baskets, around 'The redemption of Zion.' *B.M.C. Palestine*, p. 184, 2. Wt. 15·07 g. (viii, 529.)

[e] *John Hyrcanus*. Bronze, 135–104 B.C. Crested helmet. Rev. double cornucopiae, around 'Jehoḥanan the High Priest and the Commonwealth of the Jews.' *B.M.C. Palestine*, p. 188, 1. (viii, 531.)

[f], [h] *Cistophoric tetradrachms*, *ca.* 200 B.C. onwards. Cista Mystica, with half-open lid, from which a serpent issues, ivy-wreath. Rev. bow-case between two coiled serpents. [f]Minted in *Pergamum*, has monogram ΠΕΡΓ and small torch. [h] From *Ephesus*, has ΕΦΕ and a bee in wreath upon the reverse. *B.M.C. Mysia*, p. 123, 90. Wt. 12·47 g. *B.M.C. Ionia*, p. 64, 152. Wt. 12·72 g. (viii, 612.)

[g] *Rhodes*. Tetradrachm, *ca.* 300–166 B.C. Radiate head of Helios facing. Rev. rose with bud between ΡΟ; above ΤΕΙΣΥΛΟΣ (magistrate), in field statue of a goddess. *B.M.C. Caria and Islands*, p. 242, 128. Wt. 13·22 g. (viii, 633.)

14

[a]

[b]

[c]

[d]

[e]

[f]

[g]

[h]

[a] Silver obol of *Phocaea* in Ionia, sixth century B.C. Found at *Saint-Remy de Provence*. Head of a seal, a little seal beneath it (cf. *Vol. of Plates*, i, 302 [b]). Wt. 0·6 g.

[b], [c], [d] A diobol and two obols from the *Hoard of Auriol* near *Marseilles*; the type a ram's head. The first like [a] may be of Ionian mintage, the second perhaps made by a Massiliote Greek, the third is a barbarous imitation struck by the pre-Celtic inhabitants of southern France. *Bibl. Nat. Paris.* Wts. 1·15 g.; 0·6 g.; 0·6 g. (vii, 46.) See de Navarro, *Antiquity* II, 1928, p. 431.

[e]–[j] The gold stater of *Philip of Macedon* and its *Celtic derivatives*. [e] Minted by *Philip* in Macedon (cf. *Vol. of Plates*, ii, 6 [o]). [f] An intelligent *Celtic* imitation. [g] Attributed to the *Raurici* (district around Bâle); [h] to the *Aulerici Diablintes* (Normandy). [i] A type characteristic of *Kent* (but found occasionally on the opposite French coast); the head of the god with elaborately stylized hair. [j] A broken-down version of the last, hair and lines on the obverse; the horse on the reverse reduced to lines and pellets. Occurs in *S.W. England* (Oxfordshire, Sussex, Cornwall). [e] *Seltman Coll.* Wt. 8·58 g. [f] *Brit. Mus.* Wt. 8·55 g. [g] *Dessewffy Coll.* Wt. 7·43 g. [h], [i] *Brit. Mus.* Wts. 6·67 g.; 7·68 g. [j] *Dessewffy Coll.* Wt. 6 g. (vii, 46, 47.)

[k], [l], [m] Coins of the *Eastern Celts* imitated from silver tetradrachms of *Philip of Macedon* (cf. *Vol. of Plates*, ii, 6 [p]). [k] From *Pannonia*. Head of Zeus. Rev. horseman and indeterminate letters. [l] From *Dacia*. The head stylized into curves, spirals and alphabetic signs; the rider is bird-like. [m] From *Moesia*. A bearded Janiform head doubtless influenced by the Roman *as* (above, p. 6) and therefore to be dated in the second century B.C. Rev. horseman. All in the *Dessewffy Coll.* Wts. 13·45 g.; 11·10 g.; 13·52 g. (vii, 46.)

[n] Gold *Regenbogenschüsselchen* of the type attributed to the *Boii*. Bird's head, torque and pellets. Rev. concave, a 'rainbow' and six pellets. Formerly *Pozzi Coll.* Wt. 7·48 g. (vii, 47.)

[o] *Massilia.* Drachma, fourth century B.C. Head of Artemis. Rev. ΜΑΣΣΑ lion. *Brit. Mus.* Wt. 3·7 g.

[p] *Celtic imitation* of the last coin. *Dessewffy Coll.* Wt. 2·19 g. (vii, 46.)

[q] *Rhode.* Drachma; female head. Rev. open rose. *Brit. Mus.*

[r] *Emporium.* Drachma; female head, dolphin. Rev. Pegasus (cf. p. 10 [i] for a slightly later coin). *Brit. Mus.* Celtic imitations of these types are frequent. (vii, 46.)

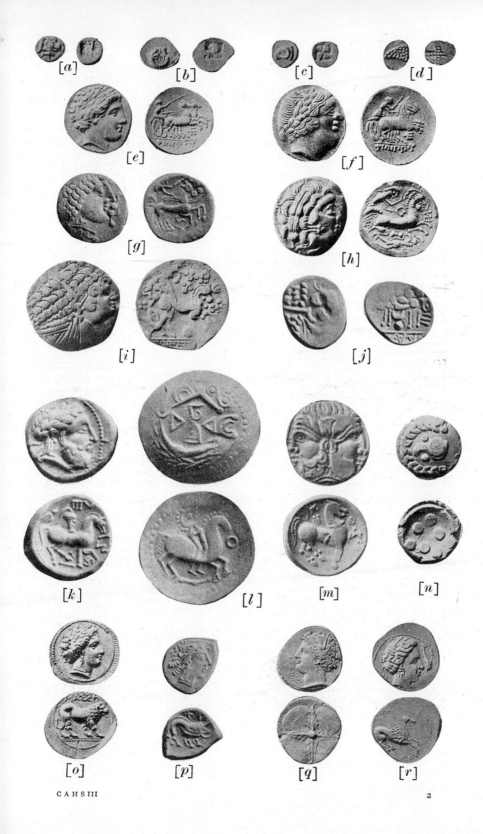

[a]　　　[b]　　　[c]　　　[d]

[e]　　　[f]

[g]　　　[h]

[i]　　　[j]

[k]　　　[l]　　　[m]　　　[n]

[o]　　　[p]　　　[q]　　　[r]

THRACIAN COINS

[a] *Sparadocus.* Tetradrachm, about 450–424 B.C. Cloaked horseman with two spears. Rev. ΣΠΑΡΑΔΟΚΟ; eagle tearing serpent. *Bibl. Nat. Paris.* Wt. 16·98 g. (On these coins [a]–[r] see viii, 556.)

[b], [c] *Seuthes I.* Silver, 424–410 B.C. Cloaked Thracian horseman. Rev. [b] ΣΕΥΘΑ ΑΡΓΥΡΙΟΝ, [c] ΣΕΝΘΑ ΚΟΜΜΑ. *Bibl. Nat. Paris.* Wt. 8·48 g. *B.M.C. Thrace*, p. 201, 1. Wt. 8·59 g.

[d], [e] *Maronea.* Bronze coins struck in the name of Thracian kings. [d] *Amatocus I*, about 405–396 B.C. Double-axe; ΑΜΑΤΟΚΟ. Rev. vine; ΕΠΙ ΚΛΕΑΝΤΟΣ (magistrate). [e] *Teres II* (about 400 B.C.). Same types, ΤΗΡΕΩ. Rev. ΕΠΙ]ΚΕΑΝΔΡ[Ο. *Sofia Mus.* and *Vienna Mus.*

[f] *Eminacus.* Silver, fifth century B.C. ΕΜΙΝΑΚΟ; Heracles in lion-skin stringing his bow. Rev. wheel and four dolphins. *Brit. Mus.*

[g] *Saratocus.* Silver, about 400 B.C. Probably minted in *Thasos.* Silen kneeling holding kantharos. Rev. ΣΑΡΑΤΟ; amphora. *Brit. Mus.* Wt. 1·11 g.

[h] *Bergaeus.* Silver, about 400–350 B.C. Perhaps minted in *Thasos.* Silen and nymph. Rev. ΒΕΡΓΑΙΟΥ. *Berlin Mus.* Wt. 3·29 g.

[i], [j], [k] *Cypsela.* Bronze coins struck for dynasts. [i] *Hebryzelmis*, 386–384 B.C. Head of city goddess. Rev. ΕΒΡΥ, a vase (*Kypsele*). [j] *Cotys I*, 384–360 B.C. Horseman. Rev. ΚΟΤΥΟΣ, a *Kypsele*. [k] *Cersobleptes*, 360–341 B.C. Female head. Rev. ΚΕΡ, a *Kypsele*. [i], [j] *Brit. Mus.* [k] *Sofia Mus.*

[l] *Cetriporis.* Bronze, about 356 B.C., probably minted in *Thasos.* Head of Dionysus. Rev. ΚΕΤΡΙΠΟΡΙΟΣ, kantharos and thyrsus. *Bibl. Nat. Paris.*

[m], [n] Bronze coins with types copied from those of *Philip of Macedon* (cf. *Vol. of Plates*, ii, 6 [p]). [m] *Scostoces*, about 350 B.C. Head of Apollo laureate. Rev. ΣΚΟΣΤΟΚΟΥ; horseman. [n] *Seuthes III*, about 338–313 B.C. Head of Zeus. Rev. ΣΕΥΘΟΥ, as last. *Sofia Mus.*

[o] *Lysimachus*, 323–281 B.C. Tetradrachm. Portrait of Alexander with horn of Ammon. Rev. ΒΑΣΙΛΕΩΣ ΛΥΣΙΜΑΧΟΥ; Athena Nikephoros (cf. *Vol. of Plates*, ii, 8 [l]). *Sofia Mus.* Wt. 17 g.

[p] *Cavarus.* Bronze, about 219–200 B.C. Head of Apollo. Rev. ΒΑΣΙΛΕΩΣ ΚΑΥΑΡΟΥ; Nike crowning his name as on Alexander's gold coins (cf. *Vol. of Plates*, ii, 8 [o]). *Sofia Mus.*

[q] *Mostis*, about 200 B.C. Tetradrachm. Portrait of king. Rev. ΒΑΣΙΛΕΩΕ ΜΟΣΤΙΔΟΣ ΕΠΙ ΣΑΔΑΛΟΥ (magistrate) ΙΓ (date year 13). *Berlin Mus.* Wt. 16·58 g.

[r] *Sadalas*, about 42 B.C. Bronze. Head of king. Rev. ΒΑΣΙΛΕΩΣ ΣΑΔΑΛΟΥ; eagle. *Sofia Mus.*

18

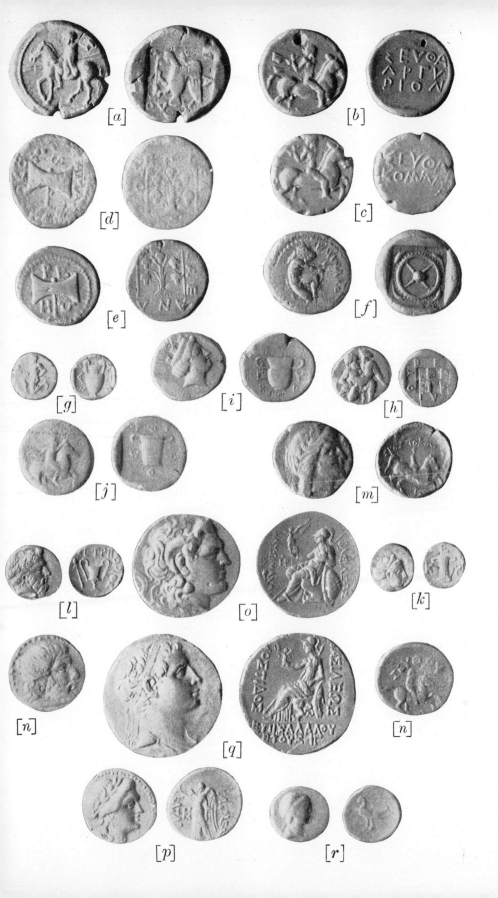

[a]

[b]

[d]

[c]

[e]

[f]

[g] [i] [h]

[j] [m]

[l] [o] [k]

[n] [q] [n]

[p] [r]

[a] *Samos*. Tetrobol, sixth century B.C. Lion's scalp facing. Rev. rough quartered incuse square. *B.M.C. Ionia*, p. 350, 1. Wt. 2·02 g. [b], [c] *Bosporan coins* imitating the Samian type. Both with facing lion's scalp. Revs. [b] ΠΑΝΤ in the four raised quarters of an incuse square; [c] ΑΠΟΛ in a quartered incuse square; the first of *Panticapaeum*, second of *Apollonia*. *Naville Catal.* v. Wt. 1·9 g. Formerly *Pozzi Coll.* Wt. 1·42 g. (viii, 562, 586.)

[d] *The Sindians*. Silver, fifth century B.C. Eagle-headed griffin with curled wing, ear of corn. Rev. ΣΙΝΔΩΝ; head of horse. *Jameson Coll.* Wt. 1·26 g. (viii, 565.)

[e]–[j] Coins of *Panticapaeum*. [e], [f] Gold staters, fourth century B.C. Heads of bearded Silens with pointed ears (cf. the heads of the Scythians on gold and silver objects, *Vol. of Plates*, i, 252, 262). Rev. ΠΑΝ; lion-headed horned griffin, with curled wing, biting a spear, ear of corn below. *Jameson Coll.* Wts. 9·09 g.; 9·09 g. [h]–[j] Silver. [h] Head as on [e]. Rev. ΠΑΝ; bull's head. [i] Facing head of beardless satyr. Rev. lion biting a spear. [j] Head of satyr. Rev. lion's head. Formerly *E. F. Weber Coll.* Wts. 3·55 g.; 2·45 g.; 2·29 g. [g] Bronze. Head of satyr. Rev. lion's head, beneath it a sturgeon. (viii, 569, 586.)

[k], [l] Coins of *Carthage*, fourth to third centuries B.C. [a] Gold stater. Head of goddess copied from Syracusan coinage (cf. p. 4 [f]). Rev. horse. *Naville Catal.* xiii. Wt. 9·38 g. [b] Bronze, similar head. Rev. horse's bust. (vii, 608; viii, 488.)

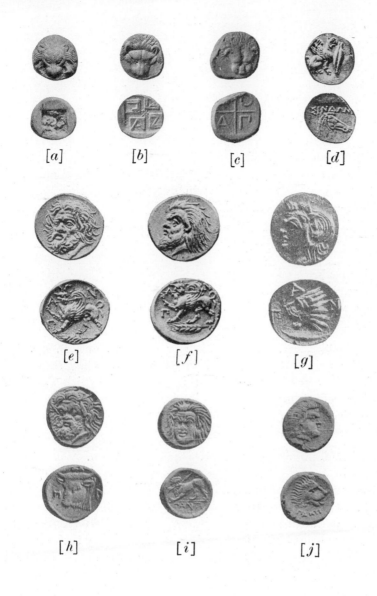

[a]   [b]   [c]   [d]

[e]   [f]   [g]

[h]   [i]   [j]

[k]   [l]

CHIEFTAIN'S GRAVE, *Weisskirchen*, Rheinprovinz, Barrow 2 La Tène A (see vii, 43 *sq.*). (*Bonner Jahrbücher*, XLIII, 1867, Pl. VII; Déchelette, *Manuel* (1914), II, 3, fig. 439; Jacobsthal and Langsdorff, *Die Bronzeschnabelkanne* (= J. and L.), 1929, p. 28, Pl. 36 *a* and *b*.)

[*a*] Bronze stamnos or vessel for mixing wine (height 40 cm.). Note beaded lip with two catches for lost lid. This vessel was found to contain white pitch. Pliny tells us that the Greeks mixed pitch, resin and other substances with their wines to give them briskness (*H.N.* XIV, 124). See de Navarro, *Antiquity*, 1928, p. 435.

[*b*] Handle with Silenus mask from same. Cf. Déchelette, *La Collection Millon* (1913), fig. 18, 3.

[*c*], [*d*] Bronze beaked flagon (*Schnabelkanne*). Height 42·5 cm. Jacobsthal (*op. cit.*) makes out a strong case for these flagons being of Etruscan, not Greek origin. They date for the most part from the opening decades of the fifth century B.C.

[*e*] Handle to same. Jacobsthal type 5 (see J. and L. pp. 45 f.). Associations of stamnoi with beaked flagons occur also on the following sites north of the Alps: Dürkheim, Rhenish Palatinate; Klein Aspergle, Wurtemberg; Weisskirchen, Barrow 2; Bouzonville, Lorraine (see p. 34). Another stamnos was found in the tumulus of La Motte St Valentin, Hte. Marne.

[*f*] Gold band, possibly an armlet. Diameter 4·7 cm. Zone of winged sphinxes in repoussé, above and below which a zone of lattice patterns between two beaded lines. Reinecke (*Mainzer Festschrift*, 1902, p. 74) considers that both in form and workmanship the sphinxes are faithful and competent copies of Greek models but that the barbaric origin of the object is betrayed by the mechanical repetition of the sphinxes and the ornamentation of the two zones framing them (vii, 48).

[*g*] Lower part of an iron dagger with remains of bronze sheath ending in a trefoil chape; note the gold foil rosettes. Length 7 cm.

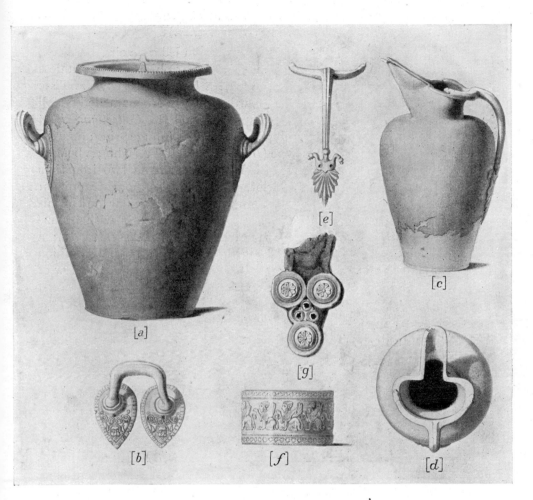

CONTENTS OF A RHENISH CHIEFTAIN'S GRAVE

THE CELTS

CHARIOT-BURIAL, *Somme Bionne, Marne.* La Tène A (see vii, 43). (*Brit. Mus. Guide, Iron Age Antiquities*[2], Pl. III; Morel, *Champagne Souterraine*, Pl. VII *sqq.* and text, pp. 23 *sqq.*; also Ebert, *Reallex. der Vorgeschichte* (= *R.L.V.*), *s.v.* Wagengrab.)

The grave in question is a flat grave, surrounded by a circular ditch. The following are among the more important objects found (unless otherwise stated they are of bronze): a long iron Early La Tène sword in a bronze and iron scabbard ending in an enamelled trefoil chape (*B.M. Guide*, fig. 54); iron spits (Déchelette, *Collection Millon* (1913), p. 231); an embossed gold band; a gold finger-ring; a girdle clasp, confronted griffons type (*B.M. Guide*, Pl. IV right); a beaked flagon (*ib.* fig. 53, cf. above, Pl. II *c*). Apart from two iron tires and other parts of the chariot, the following horse-trappings: forked objects with trefoil terminals, pierced circular and semi-circular objects (*B.M. Guide*, Pl. IV); two iron bits with bronze rings. Pottery: a local pedestal urn (*B.M. Guide*, cf. fig. 64); a red-figure Attic kylix (J. and L. Pl. 34 *a*). In Jacobsthal's opinion this vase cannot date from before 450 B.C. (*ibid.* p. 62). In view of this, the Somme Bionne chieftain was probably laid in earth between 440 and 420 B.C., possibly a generation later than the chieftain in the second Weisskirchen barrow.

Apart from relatively numerous burials in France, chariots have been found in the La Tène A Rhenish Chieftains' Graves (see also *Mannus*, XXII (1930), pp. 103 f.). For S.W. Bohemia (La Tène A), see Schraníl, *Vorgesch. Böhmens-Mährens*, p. 212. Those from Yorkshire and most of those from Hungary (*B.M. Guide*, pp. 119 *sqq.* and *R.L.V.* XIV, p. 29) date from phase C. The Yorkshire chariot-interments differ from those of the continent in that the skeletons were contracted (buried seated in the chariot?) and that horses were found: in continental chariot-burials horses are exceptional. Hallstatt chariot-graves occur from S.W. Bohemia to the Marne (Jogasses grave 16) and even further west. Unlike those of the La Tène period, many of these earlier vehicles have four wheels.

There is an allusion to chariot-burial in the 'Destruction of Dind Rig,' an Irish prose epic referring to a period prior to that of the Ulster cycle (*Zeitschrift für Celtische Philologie*, III, p. 9).

MARNE CHARIOT-BURIAL

THE CELTS

LA TÈNE A, EASTERN AREA (see vii, 43 *sq.*). (This and the following two plates are taken, respectively, from Lindenschmidt's *Altertümer unserer heidnischen Vorzeit* (= *AuhV.*), v, Pls. 50, 57, 51, which illustrate Reinecke's three papers, *ib.* pp. 281 *sqq.*, 330 *sqq.*, 288 *sqq.*, on which this text, pp. 26–30, is based. See Bibliography to Vol. VII, ch. 2, *s.v.* Lindenschmidt.)

Metal. (Unless otherwise stated the objects are bronze.)

Iron swords and scabbards with bronze chapes: [a–c] respective lengths 72 cm.; 20 cm. (length only of part illustrated); 72 cm.
Curved iron knife ('Hiebmesser')*:* [f] length, 31 cm.
Fibulae: [o]–[q] variants of the Certosa type; [w] mask-fibula; [m] bird-head fibulae; [s] stylized development of last-named type with knee bow. Lengths: 7 cm.; 7·2 cm.; 7·5 cm.; 9 cm.; 3 cm.; 4·8 cm.
Armlets: [d], [e], [u] types with three or four groups of knobs: [d] open and hollow cast, [e] and [u] closed; [l] open wire type with ring catch. Diameters: 7·5 cm.; 7·5 cm.; 7 cm.; 6·5 cm.
Torcs: [i] thin, open type, single group of knobs; [k] thin, angular in section, hook-and-eye catch; [j] thicker, cast, cast spiral ornament, and pin catch. Diameters: 14·5 cm.; 14 cm. and 15·5 cm.; 15·5 cm.

Pottery. (Monochrome; mostly dark in colour; the finer vessels in bucchero technique.)

Lenticular flasks: [r] (with zoomorphic frieze, cf. *R.L.V.* VII, Pl. 193 *d*) found with [o]–[q]; [y] and [z] with geometric ornamentation. Heights: 24 cm.; 20·5 cm.; 19 cm.
Bottle-shaped vessel: [h] rounded shoulders, broad flat base. Height: 19·5 cm.
Pail-shaped vessel: [g] 'form perhaps influenced by archaic Greek vase types (such as archaic hydria and amphora forms).' Horizontal grooves and arc motifs on neck. Height: 25 cm.
Fragment of omphalos dish: [n] the inner side decorated with curvilinear motifs. Diameter: 16·5 cm.
Vessels with everted necks and broad, elliptical bodies, on the shoulders of which are curvilinear motifs: [a_2], [c_2]. Heights: 16 cm.; 10 cm.
Vessels with everted lips and broad, more or less carinated bodies, the shoulders decorated with mouldings and geometric motifs: [t], [v], [x], [b_2]. All save [b_2] made on the wheel. Note the dragonesque motifs on [b_2]. Heights: 12·5 cm.; 12 cm.; 14·5 cm.; 17 cm.
The following have *omphalos* bases: [n], [r], [t], [v], [y], [z], [a_2]–[c_2]. For the sites on which the above objects were found see *AuhV.* v, pp. 281 *sqq.*

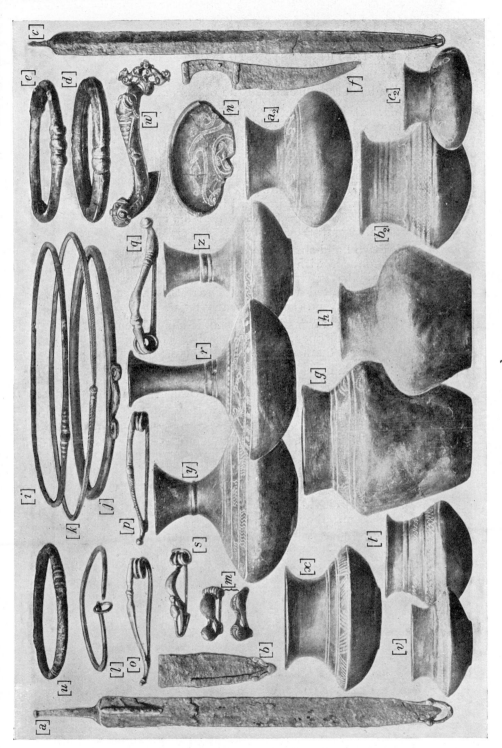

OBJECTS FROM THE LA TÈNE A EASTERN AREA

LA TÈNE B IN THE REGION TO NORTH OF THE ALPS (see vii, 44 *sq.*).

(Unless otherwise stated the objects are bronze.)

Iron swords: [a], [f] the latter with fragments of iron sheath, and chape with coral inlay. Respective lengths: 75 cm. and 70 cm.

Broken iron spear head: [b]. Length: 22·5 cm.

Fibulae: [d] foot and bow with inlay-discs; [g] iron, fragmentary; [i] with knee bow, end of foot lacking; [j] typical La Tène B form: bent-back foot touching bow; [k] bow with five borings; [l] band-shaped bow, foot lacking; [m] iron, foot with knobs; [w] red coral disc on foot. Respective lengths: 5·5 cm.; 6 cm.; 9·5 cm.; 7·5 cm.; 8 cm.; 9 cm.; 8·5 cm.; 6 cm.

Armlets: [o] two band-shaped, seal-top terminals with sunk beds for inlay; [r] knobbed, with small buffer terminals; [s] small, open, seal-top terminals; [u] fragment of large knobbed arm-ring, with *s*-motifs; [z] undulated wire type. Greatest diameters: 6·4 cm.; 7·3 cm.; 5·8 cm.; 10 cm. (length); nearly 6 cm.

Foot-rings: [v] foot- or arm-ring with saddle-shaped bend, four knobs and plug catch; [x] open, knobbed, seal-top terminals; [b_2] open, knobbed. Greatest diameters: 7 cm.; 10·5 cm.; 9·3 cm.

Torcs: [c] open, plain, seal-top terminals; [h] open, buffer terminals, coral ring-discs, etc.; [n] in two parts, buffer type, knobs, etc., with plastic decoration, plug catch; [q] closed, buffer type, plastic decoration on knobs etc., discs for inlay; [t] twisted wire, angular in section, hook-and-eye catch, glass rings on small wire rings; [c_2] plain, seal-top terminals, figurine on ring. Greatest diameters: almost 13 cm.; 15·5 cm.; 16·2 cm.; 18 cm.; 13 cm.; 13·5 cm.

Figurines (anthropomorphic): [y], [d_2], see also [c_2]. Heights: 4 cm.; 3 cm.; almost 5 cm.

Smaller rings: [e] closed, four knobs; [e_2] triannular wire object. Diameters: 3·5 cm.; about 1 cm.

Girdle-hooks: [p] hook with bronze sheet mount for end of girdle, repoussé and punched decoration; [a_2] bronze hook with rivet-holes and 'terret' for end of leather girdle. Breadths: 4 cm.; 2·8 cm.

Rattle: [f_2] clay, double conic with stamped geometric motifs. Diameter: 4·5 cm.

[a]–[e], [h], [i], [w]–[y] from *Rhenish Palatinate*; [f], [g] *Alsace*; [u] (?), [v] *Rhenish Hesse*; [q]–[t], [c_2] *Starkenburg*; [z]–[b_2] *Upper Hesse*; [n]–[p] *Hesse Nassau*; [d_2], [e_2] *Wurtemberg*; [j]–[m] *Bohemia*. For Sites, see *AuhV.* v, pp. 330 *sqq.*

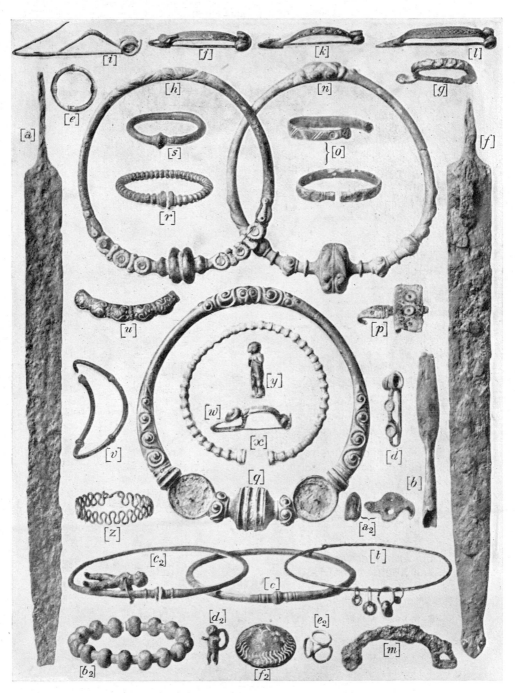

OBJECTS FROM NORTH OF THE ALPS, LA TÈNE B

THE CELTS

Metal. (Unless otherwise stated the objects are bronze.)

Iron swords: [a], [c] (with iron sheaths); [b]. Note survival of earlier (B) forms in [a] and [b]; for typical La Tène C form, cf. [c]. Respective lengths: 74 cm.; 68 cm.; 86 cm. (sheath 74 cm.).

Twisted iron sword-chain and end-piece to same: [e]. Lengths: about 48 cm.; 15 cm.

Three hollow iron sword-strap rings: [d]. Diameter: 4·5 cm.

Iron spear-heads: broad-bladed: [f] with two iron spear-butts; and [h]; narrow-bladed: [g]; [i]. Lengths: 55 cm. (length of butts: 9 cm.; 11 cm.); 30 cm.; 33 cm.; 43 cm.

Iron shield boss: [j] 'trigger-guard' form and two iron 'shield-bindings.' Lengths: 33 cm.; 19 cm.; 17·5 cm.

Iron shears: [x]. Length: 23 cm.

Tweezer: [y]. Length: 5·7 cm.

Fibulae: [u], [v] (both iron), typical La Tène C forms (foot clasping bow); [w], [i_2] pseudo-La Tène B fibulae. Lengths: 11·2 cm.; 17 cm.; 7·9 cm.; 16 cm.

Armlets: [n] closed deep blue glass outer side with three rows of points; [o] hollow bossed type (*Nussarmring*) with hinge (arm- or foot-ring); [p] ditto, but larger bosses (arm-ring); [q] spiral wire, with two blue glass beads with orange yellow spirals, and zigzags; [r] closed, fluted, three rectangular plaques; [s] closed, three groups of pronounced triple knobbing; [t] open, 'cast torsion'; [g_2] closed, lignite. Greatest diameters: 9 cm.; about 12 cm.; 9·5 cm.; 6 cm.; 9 cm.; 8·3 cm.; 6·3 cm.; 7 cm.

Torc: [k] iron, 'omega' torc, button terminals. Greatest diameter: 17 cm.

Girdles, etc: [l] clasp- and suspension-hooks with pendants from big girdle-chain of ring, rod and cruciform members, red enamel on last-named and clasp-hook. Hooks with zoomorphic heads (cf. *AuhV.* v, p. 288, fig. 1); [m] end-pieces (zoomorphic clasp-hook and pendants) of a doubled girdle-chain (cf. *ib.*); [h_2] parts of a girdle-chain (on zoomorphic clasp-hook and end-piece, red enamel inlay). Total lengths of chains: about 154 cm.; 172 cm.; 123 cm.

Pottery. (Asterisk denotes wheel-made.)

Monochrome grey to grey-black ware: [z] bowl, incurving lip (diameter about 18 cm.); *[a_2] pedestal vase (height 20·5 cm.); *[b_2] pail-shaped vessel, curved profile, moulding on shoulder (height 26·5 cm.); *[c_2] pail-shaped vessel, strongly curved profile, moulding on shoulder (height 16·5 cm.); *[d_2] brown pedestal vase, curved profile (height 23 cm.); [e_2] pot, channelled walls, convex profile (height 16·5 cm.); [f_2] flat, sharp-angled dish (height 4·6 cm.); [j_2] pail-shaped, biconic vessel, channelled walls, stamped concentric circles on shoulder (height 12·5 cm.); [k_2] biconic vessel, foot-ring, moulding and grooves on shoulder (height 20 cm.).

[a] from *Straubing*; [b]–[f_2] *Manching*; [g_2]–[k_2] *Aislingen*.

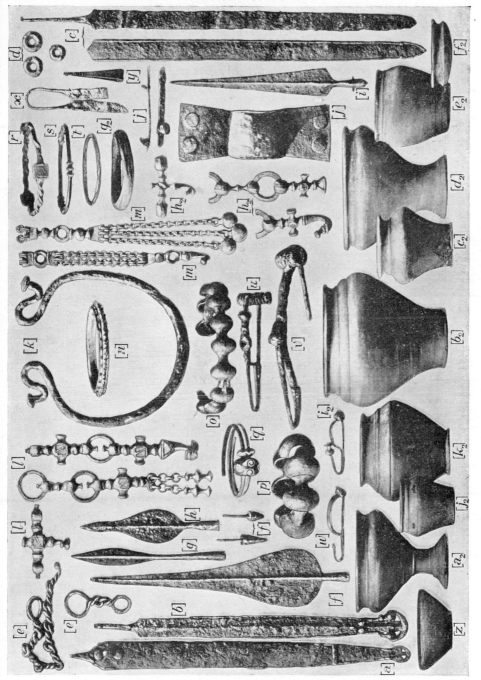

OBJECTS FROM THE BAVARIAN DANUBE VALLEY, LA TÈNE C

THE CELTS

EXAMPLES OF LA TÈNE A ORNAMENTATION FROM THE
MIDDLE RHINE AND MARNE AREAS (see vii, 47 *sq.*).

[a] Gold pierced mounting, possibly for a cup, from a Chieftain's Grave at Schwarzenbach (Barrow 1), Birkenfeld (= *Bonner Jahrbücher*, XXIII, Pl. IV, 3; cf. Baldes-Behrens, *Katalog Birkenfeld*, Pl. 5). The top frieze, framed by zones of beading, is mainly composed of 'Celtic' (three-leaved) and disintegrated palmettes. The middle, of stylized palmettes, the multifoliate articulation of their two lower side leaves contributing to the formation of the palmette derivatives with which they alternate. The lowest and narrowest frieze is composed of bud motifs, the neck of each bud being separated by a moulding from the crest of the undulated line on which it stands (cf. Déchelette, *Manuel*, fig. 664); two zones of beading.

[b] Engraved ornamentation on the bronze helmet from Berru, Marne (= *Rev. Archéologique*, 1875, I, Pl. X; cf. Déchelette, *op. cit.* figs. 656 and 490.2). (See vii, 48.) Top left hand corner: interlocking *s*-motifs with foliate 'insets.' Top right hand corner and middle: derivatives from the enclosed palmette alternately inverted and connected by curved almond-shaped motifs; on the projecting parts, palmette derivatives and palmettes. Lowest: degenerate derivatives of the enclosed palmette; similar connecting motifs. The engravings on this helmet (with which cf. Déchelette, *op. cit.* fig. 655) reveal a tendency towards a treatment of design fundamentally at variance with classical tradition: the abolition of the distinction between the pattern and its background, brought about by the covering of a given ornamental field with primary and complementary motifs. Not only did this practice open a whole range of fantastic curvilinear patterns, but it contributed very largely to the abstract, geometric treatment of ultimately naturalistic motifs. The origin of this innovation is perhaps to be sought in pierced metalwork (cf. [a]), or possibly in such inlay work as that on the throats of the Bouzonville flagons (cf. p. 35). On the helmet from Berru the contrast is heightened by the complementary motifs being carried out in *pointillé*. For an example of developed primary and complementary ornamentation, see the bronze mirror from Desborough (*B.M. Iron Age Guide*, fig. 133).

[a]

[b]

EXAMPLES OF LA TÈNE A ORNAMENTATION

BRONZE BEAKED FLAGON of Celtic workmanship from *Bouzonville*, near *Metz*. La Tène A. In the *British Museum*. (R. A. Smith, *Celtic Bronzes from Lorraine*, in *Archaeologia*, LXXIX, pp. 1 *sqq.*; *Illustrated London News*, March 23rd and 30th, 1929; *The British Museum Quarterly*, IV, No. 3, p. 66; J. and L. p. 99.) One of a pair of bronze flagons (*oinochoai*) ornamented with coral and red enamel, found with two bronze stamnoi (cf. above, p. 23 [a]). Greatest height: about 39·4 cm. Patina, a dark lustrous green. For a full description of this remarkable flagon see Smith, *op. cit.* pp. 3 *sqq.* (cf. *ib.* fig. 4). The flagons from Bouzonville differ in many features from the usual type of *oinochoe* (cf. above, p. 23 [c], [d]): the bodies of the former are tall and high-shouldered and only paralleled by the clay *Schnabelkanne* from Hallstatt (J. and L. p. 99, Pl. 27, No. 138); the beaks and the tops of the Bouzonville vessels are covered in (the wine was poured in through a narrow hole, closed with an enamelled bronze stopper, and out through a narrow tube, the point of egress lying below the duck on the spout). They also differ in being embellished with coral and red enamel, and in certain of their zoomorphic features: the duck on the covered spout, the ear- and thigh-spirals on the beasts. The latter features have been attributed to Scythian influence (but see J. and L. p. 59 for thigh-spirals). Should this view prove correct, the occurrence of such spirals on the Bouzonville flagons—which also bear very early Celtic enamel work—would lend colour to the view that the art of enamelling reached the Celtic area from the Black Sea region. Owing to the dearth of connecting links, it is not easy to determine the routes by which Scythian influence reached the Celtic area during La Tène A: although there is undeniable evidence for the presence of Scythian raiders in Silesia during the fifth century (see *Schlesiens Vorzeit*, N.F. IX, pp. 11 *sqq.*), the Celtic invasion of that region did not occur until phase B of the La Tène period. Ear-spirals are foreign to Greek and Etruscan art; but, in comparing resemblances between the Scythian and Celtic styles, one should not forget that they were both to a great extent parallel but independent barbaric developments of a common classical influence (vii, 48). Although this important new find may reveal the existence of Scythian influence upon Celtic Art as early as La Tène A, there is no reason to believe that influence to have been of other than secondary importance.

BRONZE FLAGON FROM LORRAINE

3-2

OBJECTS from the DOUBLE BURIAL near *Waldalgesheim, Huns-rück*. La Tène B (vii, 45) (= *R.L.V.* XIV, Pl. 55–6; E. aus'm Weerth, *Der Grabfund von W., Bonner Winckelmannsprogramm*, 1870; *Führer durch das Provinzialmuseum, Bonn* (1915), p. 25, Pl. 9 (1, 2), Pl. 10; Behrens, *Katalog Bingen* (1918), pp. 25 *sqq.*). The lower of the two graves contained the remains of a man with his horse, chariot, table service [a], [b], etc.; the upper one that of his wife or concubine with rich objects of adornment (see [c]–[f]). (Cf. vii. 73.)

[a] The bronze flagon is a Celtic derivation from the earlier Etruscan *Schnabelkanne*. Instead of a beak it is furnished with a tubular spout, and differs still further from the usual beaked flagon in the shape of its body and its foot (cf. 23 [c]). The small horse surmounting the vessel in the photograph is thought to belong to the lid. Note the bearded figure with human ears and long pointed ears (horns?) at the foot of the handle, probably derived from the Achelous mask. For the ornamentation on the body of the vessel, not visible on this plate, see *B.M. Iron Age Guide*, fig. 11, p. 20 (cf. *Mainzer Festschr.* 1902, p. 82; J. and L. p. 44). Further examples of this type of flagon occur in France (2) and the Rhenish Palatinate (1), while a number of imitations in pottery came to light in the South Swiss (Ticino) cemeteries (cf. Behrens, *op. cit.* p. 28 *sq.*; Déchelette, *op. cit.* II, 3, fig. 654, p. 1454 *sq.*).

[b] The bronze bucket is one of the only Greek works of art found in the transalpine Celtic area in a La Tène B context (cf. vii, 45). Outside of that area, apart from the example cited on vii, 45, one of these buckets was found at Kjeldby (Denmark). Cf. Déchelette, *op. cit.* pp. 1440–2. The free flower-tendrils (*frei bewegte Blüthenranken*) at the base of the drooping palmette on the Waldalgesheim bucket show that this vessel cannot be dated earlier than the closing years of the fifth century B.C. (cf. *Mainzer Festschr.* 1902, p. 81).

[c] Gold torc with buffer terminals. The ornamentation (forked flower-tendrils) is directly derived from the decoration on the bucket [b]. For full analysis of the ornamentation, see *B.M. Iron Age Guide*, pp. 19 *sqq.*

[d], [e] Two gold buffer-ended wristlets decorated with human masks, palmette decorations, free tendril motifs, etc.

[f] Closed, twisted gold ring for the upper arm.

The chief new classical contribution towards La Tène B art is the free tendril motif.

[a]   [b]

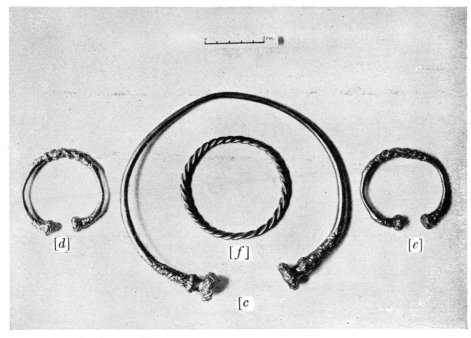

[d]   [f]   [e]

[c]

OBJECTS FROM WALDALGESHEIM

Types of BRONZE AGE CHIP-CARVED POTTERY, *Kerbschnitt-keramik* (= *RLV*. VIII, pl. 78). (vii, 55.) [a]–[b] From *Bavaria*. [c]–[g] From *Wurtemberg*. [h]–[i] From *Hesse*. Respective heights: 12·5 cm.; 8 cm.; 6 cm.; 5 cm.; 10·5 cm.; 12 cm.; 5·7 cm.; 8·5 cm.; 13·8 cm. Apart from the Lower Rhenish area chip-carved pottery practically disappears in Hallstatt A to re-emerge in Hallstatt C (see vii, 55 on recrudescence of the Bronze Age population in South Germany). Also cf. forms of funnel-neck globular-bodied vessels of Hallstatt B (*AuhV*. v, Nos. 1002, 1007) with fig. [f] and Behrens, *Bronzezeit Süddeutschlands*, Pl. XV). See Behrens, *op. cit.* for sites.

HARPSTEDT POTTERY (= *Mannus*, XVII (1926), p. 293). (See vii, 67, 56.)

The cradle of the Harpstedt style lay in the region between the Ems and the Weser, whence it spread [i] through the Lippe valley to the Lower Rhenish area, [ii] through Brunswick to East Havelland and parts of Saxony. The vessels, which vary in colour (light yellow, reddish, dark brown), are more or less pail-shaped with frilled lips and rough walls; the roughened appearance is obtained by smearing, or combing. According to Stampfuss' revised chronology (cf. *Mannus*, Ergänzungsband v (1927), pp. 50 *sqq.* with *Mannus*, XVII, 1926, pp. 287 *sqq.*), the vessels date from Northern Bronze Age V to Hallstatt C. Rhenish variants [t]–[u], often with finger-tip ornamentation, occur in the Middle Rhenish zone (cf. Rittershausen, *Nass.Annalen*, 1926, Pl. IX, 12, 13, and the Coblentz region, *Mannus*, XXII, 1930, p. 109 *sq.*), where they overlap with the Mehren (Hallstatt C/D) and La Tène A cultures. The people who brought these vessels with them to the Lower Rhine area are held to be the first Teutonic invaders to settle in those parts.

Type I, [j]–[k], does not survive the Bronze Age; type II, [l]–[m], is more frequently found in the Bronze Age; types III, IV, V, [n]–[o], [p]–[q], [r]–[s], date from Hallstatt C, although a few examples of type III occur in Bronze Age V. Certain vessels of true Hallstatt C/D forms found in the Lower Rhenish area reveal in the roughening of their walls Harpstedt influence. (See Stampfuss, the two papers referred to above, and literature there cited; Kendrick, *The Druids*, p. 39 *sq.*, for occurrence in England; cf. Childe, *The Danube*, p. 364 *sq.*)

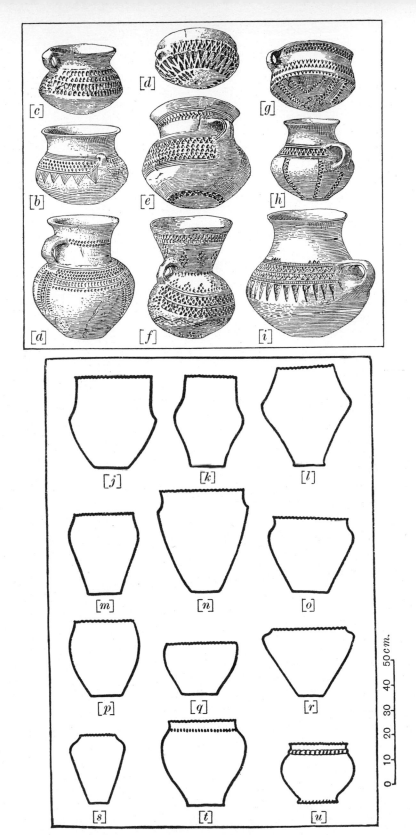

TYPES OF POTTERY

POTTERY FROM THE LOWER RHINE AND THE MARNE.
[a], [b] *Pail-shaped urns* (Eimerurnen) *with 'finger-nail' ornamentation*. [a] from *Hirzenberg* near *Siegburg*, Rhine Province; *Hallstatt* D (= *R.L.V.* VIII, Pl. 161 *c*). [b] from *Marson*, Marne; La Tène I (= *B.M. Iron Age Guide*, Pl. V 8). Height: 16 cm.

[c], [d] *Broad paunched urns with tall incurving necks*. [c] with triangular motifs on paunch, from *Hirzenberg* near *Siegburg*; Hallstatt D (= *R.L.V.* VIII, Pl. 161 *f*). Also found in Mehren (Hallstatt C/D) contexts (vii, 69). [d] slightly carinated variant of same, with decoration in white, from *Haulzy*, Marne, grave 78; beginning of the La Tène period (= Goury, *L'Enceinte d'Haulzy*...Pl. IV). Height: 22·5 cm. Further examples of this type occur at Étrechy, Marne (Morel, *op. cit.* Pl. 19. 9 and 12). Cf. also Baldes-Behrens, *Katalog Birkenfeld*, Pl. XII 9, and the more angular La Tène I variants from the Trèves region (Déchelette, *op. cit.* fig. 669). [a], [c] *Cologne Museum*, [b] *Brit. Mus.*, [d] Nancy Museum.

The distribution of these types of pottery supports E. Rademacher's view of a migration of part of the Lower Rhenish 'Tumulus peoples' into the Marne and Middle Rhine areas at the end of Hallstatt D (*R.L.V.* V, s.v. *Haulzy*, and VIII, p. 497); (see also vii, 67 *sq.*). Haulzy was cited (vii, 60) as an isolated link between the Lower Rhenish Tumulus peoples and the Late Hallstatt Celtic invaders of Spain. Since the publication of vol. VII, other sites of the Haulzy type have been excavated by Chenet in the east Marne district. Apart from these, Hallstatt influences reached the Marne (*Rev. Arch.* 1927, Jogasses) presumably from the Swiss plateaux. What is probably an earlier type of the Siegburg-Haulzy urn was found at Can Missert (Terassa), Catalonia (*Anuari de l'Institut d'Estudis Catalans*, VI, p. 584, fig. 335; still closer parallels are to be seen in the Barcelona museum). Kraft and Bosch Gimpera (*Mannus*, Ergbd. VI (1928), pp. 258 *sqq.*) and Kraft (*Stellung der Schweiz*...in *Anzeiger f. Schweiz. Altertumskunde*, 1927/8, and *Antiquity*, 1929, pp. 33 *sqq.*) show that there is reason to believe that the Celts invaded coastal Catalonia as early as the Urnfield Period (vii, 55). These papers, which only came into the writer's hands after vol. VII, chap. II, was in the Press, are important. Nevertheless, the location of the early home of the Celts in the Rhone area is not borne out by the testimony of river-names [vii, 54]. Further, 1100 B.C. seems too early a date for this invasion: in spite of the occurrence of cylinder-neck urns, other types of pottery from Can Missert and similar sites point to the event in question not taking place prior to Hallstatt B, circ. 900–800 B.C., and possibly being connected with Hallstatt pressure on the Swiss lake-dwelling population. The finds from Peralada show that Catalonia was also affected by the Late Hallstatt Celtic invasions (*Anuari*, VI, p. 590 *sq.*; cf. vii, 59 *sq.*).

[c]   [a]

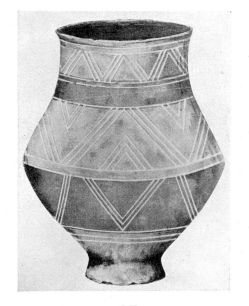

[d]   [b]

POTTERY FROM THE LOWER RHINE AND THE MARNE

SPAIN

IBERIAN POTTERY from South-eastern *Spain, Aragon.*

[*a*], [*b*] Bowls from *Sant Antoni* near *Calaceite*: [*a*] diameter: 21 cm.; [*b*] diameter: 26 cm.

[*c*]–[*f*] Goblets and bowls from *Azáila* in *Saragossa*: [*c*] height: 20 cm.; [*d*] height: 22·5 cm.; [*e*] diameter: 25 cm.; [*f*] diameter: 24 cm.

This pottery owes much to Greek influences. (vii, 785.)

[M. Ebert, *Reallexikon der Vorgeschichte*, x]

[a]

[b]

[c]

[d]

[e]

[f]

IBERIAN POTTERY

SPAIN

IBERIAN WEAPONS

[*a*] An iron *Pilum*, 70 cm. long. [*b*] An iron sword, *Falcata*, 57·4 cm. long. [*c*] Sword, La Tène C type. *Gladius Hispaniensis*, 68·6 cm. long. All from the cemetery at *Cabrera de Mataró*, Province of *Barcelona*. (vii, 784; viii, 86.)

[M. Ebert, *Reallexikon der Vorgeschichte*, x]

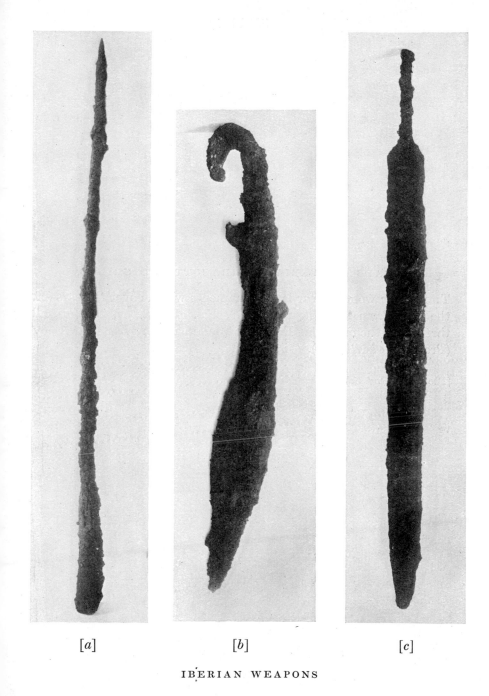

[a]   [b]   [c]

IBERIAN WEAPONS

HEADS OF IBERIAN TERRACOTTA FIGURINES

Two of the women wear large ornaments which cover the ears (cf. the head from *Elche* near *Alicante*, *Vol. of Plates*, i, 294 [*b*]), all three wear the mantilla. From the Iberian site *Serreta* near Alcoy (Province of *Alicante*). (vii, 785.)

[*Photograph Prof. Schulten*]

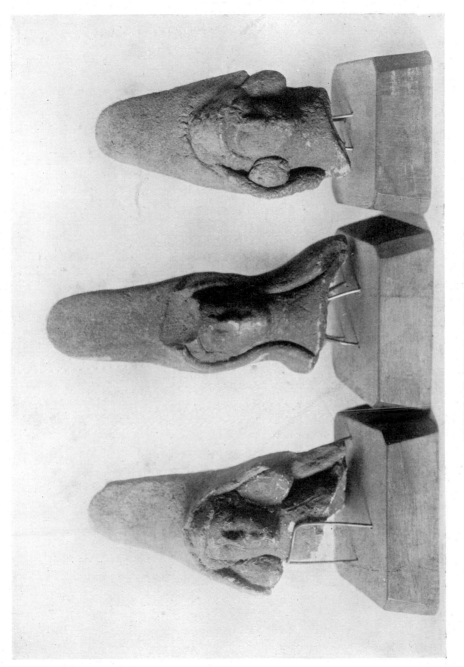

IBERIAN TERRACOTTA HEADS

[a] Part of THE ROMAN CIRCUMVALLATION of *Numantia*. In the foreground, marked by an arrow, appears part of Scipio's vallum. (viii, 321.)

[b] HEADQUARTERS OF SCIPIO on *Castillejo* to the north-west of *Numantia*. The picture shows a room with six column-bases in the *praetorium* of Marcellus. (viii, 321.)

[*A. Schulten*, Numantia, III, Pl. 3, 1; Pl. 14, 2]

[a] A PART OF THE CIRCUMVALLATION OF NUMANTIA

[b] HEADQUARTERS OF SCIPIO

Two views of the HOUSE OF THE FAUN at *Pompeii*. Second century B.C.

[*a*] The large *atrium*.

[*b*] The two Corinthian columns of the *tablinum* in which was found the Alexander mosaic (cf. *Vol. of Plates*, ii, 110). The 'incrustation' type of mural decoration appears on either side of the *tablinum*. (viii, 347.)

[a]

[b]

HOUSE OF THE FAUN, POMPEII

[*a*] From an Attic red-figure column-crater by the Orpheus painter, found at *Gela*, now in *Berlin*. Orpheus singing to the accompaniment of his lyre, surrounded by Thracians; they wear long embroidered cloaks and fox-skin caps. Two lances are carried by each Thracian. (viii, 543, 544.)

[A. Furtwängler, *Kleine Schriften*, ii, Pl. 50.]

[*b*] Fragment of an Attic white-ground kylix by the Pistoxenos painter, found on the Acropolis in *Athens*. A Thracian woman; an animal appears tattooed on her arm. (viii, 543.)

[E. Pfuhl, *Malerei und Zeichnung der Griechen*, iii, 416. F. Bruckmann A. G., Munich.]

[a]

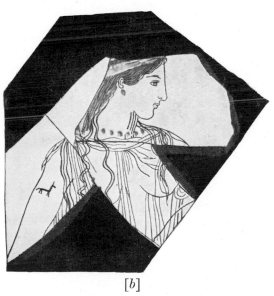

[b]

THRACIANS ON ATTIC VASES

[*a*] Relief of the fourth century B.C. Bendis, wearing a long-sleeved shortened chiton, covered by an animal's skin (*nebris*) slung over the left shoulder. A long cloak (*zeira*) falls behind, on her head a Thracian cap and on her feet high boots with tops turned over. Her right hand holds a patera, her left a spear. Facing her are two bearded men in chitons, the leader carrying a torch in his lowered right hand. They are followed by eight naked epheboi. In the *British Museum*. (viii, 549.)

[*b*] Relief from *Shapla-dere* (Mesembria on the coast of the Aegean). A four-wheeled cart drawn by a pair of mules or horses. The driver, wearing a sleeved chiton and cloak, sits on the box. In the cart behind is a passenger wearing a cloak clasped in front. An outrider, wearing short chiton and cloak, precedes the cart. About 450 B.C. Height 1·02 m. *Sofia National Museum*. (viii, 555.)

[*c*] A funeral stele from *Abdera*. A horseman wearing chiton, chlamys and baggy trousers riding to right; on his right hip, hung from a belt, is a sword, and his right hand once brandished a spear. His left arm raises an oval shield. Behind him (much mutilated) stands the figure of a soldier carrying two spears. Second to first century B.C. Height 1·23 m. *Sofia National Museum*. (viii, 543.)

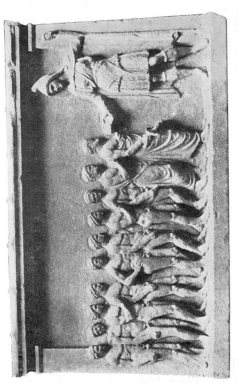

[a]

[b]

[c]

RELIEFS DEPICTING THRACIAN COSTUME

[*a*] BRONZE HELMET, Thracian shape, with cheek-pieces, from a grave near *Kovatshovitsa* (district of *Nevrokop* in northern Macedonia). Fourth century B.C. Height 39 cm. *Sofia Nat. Mus.* (viii, 546.)

[*b*] THRACIAN BRONZE HELMET found near *Karaagačh* (district of *Philippopolis*). Fourth century B.C. (?). *Sofia Nat. Mus.* (viii, 546.)

[*c*] IRON CURVED SWORD found near *Vinograd* (district of *Gorna-Orechovitza*, northern Bulgaria); La Tène type. Length 40 cm. *Sofia Nat. Mus.* (viii, 545.)

[a]

[b]

[c]

ARMS AND ARMOUR

[*a*] SILVER CHAIN from *Bukyovtsi* (district of *Orechovo* in northern Bulgaria). Attached to the chain are five (originally six) fibulae, each 8·5 cm. long. The chains depend from rosettes with heads (perhaps of Apollo) beneath them. From the shorter chains hang pellets shaped like poppy-heads.

[*b*] DECORATED SILVER VASE of oinochoe type, with tall foot and wide lip. Height 15 cm.

[*c*] SMALL SILVER VASE without decoration. Height 6·4 cm.

All in *Sofia Nat. Mus.* (viii, 557.)

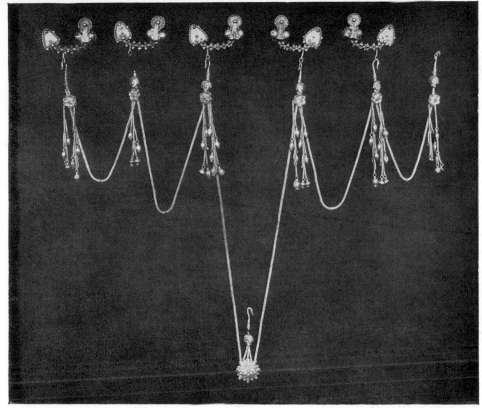

[a]

[b]

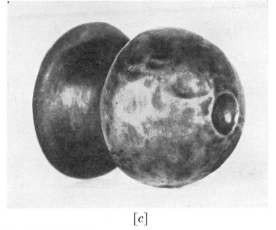

[c]

OBJECTS IN SILVER

[a] On the left a SILVER FIBULA, length 5·9 cm., engraved, from the district of *Vratsa* in northern Bulgaria; on the right another, length 4·5 cm., from a tumulus near *Tsareva-Livada* (district of *Gabrovo* in northern Bulgaria). La Tène A.

[b] POTTERY FUNERAL URN with four handles from *Pashaköi* (district of *Kizilagač* in southern Bulgaria). On it are incised four stylized animals, the one illustrated having upon its flank a design resembling the fibulae above [a]. La Tène. Height 29 cm.

All in *Sofia Nat. Mus.* (viii, 557.)

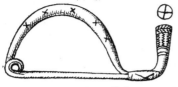

[a] SILVER FIBULA

[b] FUNERAL URN

[a] MASSIVE GOLD RING with swivelling bezel bearing an engraved Thracian inscription in Greek characters:

ΡΟΛΙΣΤΕΝΕΑΣΝ|ΕΡΕΝΕΑΤΙΛ|ΤΕΑΝΗΣΚΟΑ|
ΡΑΣΕΑΔΟΜ|ΕΑΝΤΙΛΕΣΥ ΠΤΑΜΙΗΕ|ΡΑΣ|ΗΛΤΑ

From a tumulus near *Ezerovo* (district of *Borissovgrad*, southern Bulgaria). Fifth century B.C. Weight 31·3 grammes; the bezel 20 × 17 mm. *Sofia Nat. Mus.* (viii, 554.)

[b] TWO GOLD RINGS (diam. 2·3 cm.) with oval bezels. The one on the left is engraved with the design of a cock: the other was probably once enamelled, the ends of the hoop terminating in serpents' heads. Weights 16·2; 15·45 g.

[c] MASSIVE GOLD ARMLET ending in serpents' heads. Diam. 9 cm. Wt. 298·25 g.

[d] GOLD PENDANT, the central portion of a necklace.

[e] SILVER AMPHORA originally covered in gold-leaf; the lower portion fluted, around the shoulder a double zone of lotus-leaves linked together by volute-like stalks. The handles are winged Persian lion-griffins (cf. the Persian silver-gilt handle, *Vol. of Plates*, i, 324 [d]). The vase is perhaps of Ionian workmanship. Height 27 cm.

[b]–[e] from the tumulus near *Duvanli* in southern Bulgaria (cf. p. 64). Fifth century B.C. *Sofia Nat. Mus.* (viii, 557.)

[a]

[b]

[c]

[d]

[e]

OBJECTS IN GOLD AND SILVER

[a] GOLD TORC of stout twisted wire, diam. 12·8 cm.; wt. 349 g.; hollow gold pyramidal pendant, height 2·5 cm.; and gold earring, diam. 2·5 cm., the thicker portion hollow.

[b] A pair of FISH of thin gold plate. Length 31·5, 28·2 cm. Wts. 45, 50 g. *Philippopolis Nat. Mus.* (viii, 557.)

All from the tumulus near *Duvanli* (cf. p. 62).

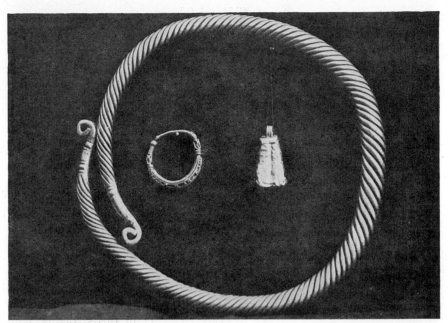

[a] GOLD TORQUE

[b] GOLD FISH

[*a*] SILVER JUG with handle and curved lip; round the shoulder runs an engraved band of vertical lines. Height 9 cm.

[*b*] SILVER PHALERA in repoussé work; Heracles strangling the Nemean lion. Diam. 8·8 cm.

[*c*] On the left, two HORSE-TRAPPINGS of silver heavily alloyed with copper. The upper specimen (length 6·5 cm.) consists of two lion's hind-legs (cf. 70 [*a*]), the paws ending in birds' heads, while the flank has a griffin's head upon it, the whole being framed in a cable border. The lower specimen (length 6·1 cm.) is shaped like a pair of fantastic monsters. On the right, a convex bronze ornament of SPIRALS and a PALMETTE, probably from the base of the handle of a bronze jug. Height 5·3 cm.

All from the tumulus near *Panagyurishte* (cf. p. 68). *Sofia Nat. Mus.* (viii, 558, 573.)

[a]   [b]

OBJECTS IN SILVER

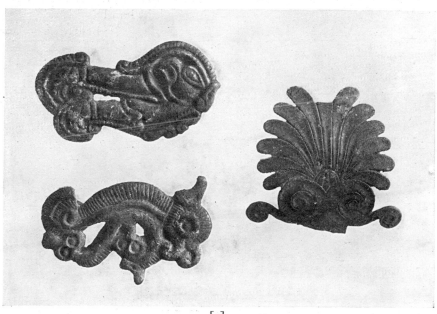

[c]

ORNAMENTS OF SCYTHIAN TYPE

[*a*] Three SILVER PHALERAE in repoussé work; on the first a rosette consisting of five lotus-buds (diam. 8·6 cm.); the others (diam. 8 cm.) engraved with a pair of symmetrically grouped animals (perhaps pigs); behind them is a bird and before them a palmette springing from a dotted volute.

[*b*] THIN SILVER PLATE shaped like a double-axe (probably a horse's frontlet): in the centre is a large rosette, above is Heracles, in barbarian garb, holding a club in his right hand and leading with his left an animal (the Nemean lion or Cerberus?); beneath him and under the rosette are two winged griffin-like monsters; at the bottom appears a siren with a lyre. Length 32 cm.

All from the tumulus near *Panagyurishte* (cf. p. 66). *Sofia Nat. Mus.* (viii, 558.)

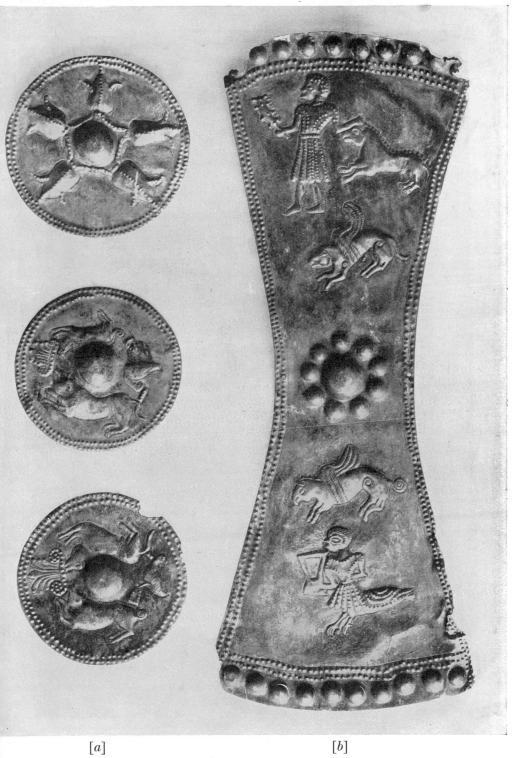

SILVER ORNAMENTS

[a] Above, a pair of SILVER ORNAMENTS, length 7·2 cm., in the form of stylized lion's hind-legs grown together (cf. 66 c). Below, a pair of griffin's heads, lengths 4·5, 4·8 cm. From the tumulus near *Brezovo*. Fourth to third century B.C.

[b] SILVER BOWL with central boss, diam. 10 cm., and a SILVER ORNAMENT, similar to those described above, length 6·5 cm. From *Radyuvene*, fourth to third century B.C.

[c] BRONZE BUCKET with ring-base and double-handle; an egg-and-tongue moulding runs round under the rim; the attachments for the handles are decorated with palmettes. From *Brezovo*. Height 22 cm.

[d], [e] Two SILVER ORNAMENTS worked *à jour*. [d] A design of interlinking spirals and circles round a central boss. Height 6·3 cm. [e] A long-necked stylized animal (horse or reindeer). 5 cm. across. From *Brezovo*.

All in *Sofia Nat. Mus.* (viii, 558, 573.)

[a]

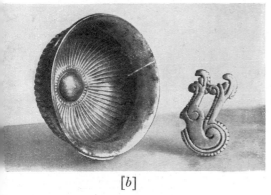

[b]

[c]

[d]

[e]

OBJECTS OF GREEK AND SCYTHIAN TYPE

[*a*] Two IRON SPEAR-HEADS and the SHEATH of a CURVED SWORD from *Vinograd*. Lengths 40·5 cm.; 37 cm.; 17·5 cm. La Tène (cf. p. 28 [*b*]).

[*b*] The upper part of a LONG IRON SWORD, length 38 cm., and the fragment of a SHEATH from a grave near *Popitsa* (district of *Bela-Slatina* in northern Bulgaria) (cf. p. 30 [*c*]).

[*c*] IRON BIT from *Vinograd*. Length 23 cm. La Tène.

[*d*] BRONZE FIBULA, length 8·6 cm., from the district of *Tirnovo* in northern Bulgaria. La Tène.

[*e*] IRON SPUR, width 9·6 cm., from *Vinograd*.

[*f*] IRON FIBULA, length 11·7 cm., found near *Pleven* in northern Bulgaria. La Tène C (cf. p. 30 [*u*], [*v*]).

All in *Sofia Nat. Mus.* (viii, 560.)

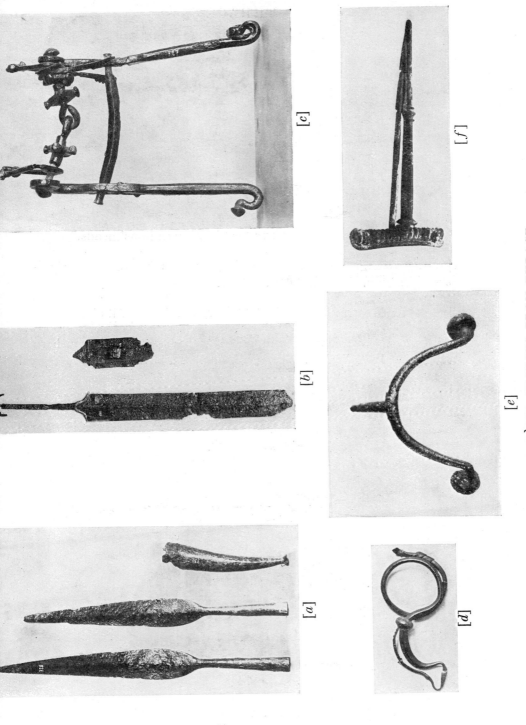

LA TÈNE OBJECTS FROM THRACE

[*a*] A pair of GOLD EARRINGS terminating in lions' heads.

[*b*] ORNAMENT of twisted silver wire, the ends decorated with lyre-shaped plates. Length 23 cm.

[*c*], [*d*] A BRONZE JUG, height 11 cm., and detail of its handle.

All from a grave near *Kran* in the district of *Kazanlik* in southern Bulgaria. In *Sofia Nat. Mus.* (viii, 560.) La Tène B.

[*After drawings by R. Popov*]

[a]

[b]

[c]

[d]

OBJECTS FROM KRAN

A set of three SILVER-GILT PHALERAE in high relief; each has a triple frame consisting of a coarse leaf border, a striped border and a raised cable border.

[a] A horseman wearing trousers, top-boots and a stiff cloak, round his neck a collar of five spirals. He raises his right hand in a gesture of adoration (cf. *Vol. of Plates*, i, 264). Diam. 15·5 cm.

[b] Female bust facing. Two plaits of her thick hair hang down in front of her shoulders; round her neck is a collar of eight spirals and she wears armlets, each of five spirals, with triangular ornaments above and below each armlet; she is clad in a sleeveless woollen tunic with embroidered border, a plait (perhaps a gold ornament?) hangs between the breasts. Over each shoulder appears a bird (dove?). Diam. 18·3 cm.

[c] Elaborate rosette with central sunflower ornament. Diam. 12·5 cm. [cf. Rostovtzeff, *Recueil Kondakoff*, Pls. XXIII, XXIV; and p. 110 below].

All from *Galiče* (district of *Orechovo* in northern Bulgaria). *Sofia Nat. Mus.* (viii, 560.) Second to first century B.C.

[a]

[b]

[c]

SILVER-GILT PHALERAE

ENGRAVED and GILT SILVER MIRROR, probably imported from Aeolian Asia Minor. Greek workmanship. Found in a Scythian barrow-grave near *Kelermes* in the Kuban region. Adorned with various figures of gods and animals, the most prominent being the winged figure of the Great Goddess, mistress of animals, the πότνια θηρῶν, and opposite it a group of two Silens (forest-spirits) fighting a griffin. Sixth century B.C. In the *Hermitage*. (viii, 571.)

[Rostovtzeff, *Iranians and Greeks*, Pl. VI; Ebert, *Reallexikon der Vorgeschichte*, VI, p. 279, Pl. 81 *a*]

SILVER MIRROR

[a] GOLD CUP of Assyro-Phoenician or early Persian workmanship. Found in a Scythian barrow-grave near *Kelermes* in the Kuban region. Decorated with three rows of animals in repoussé work: a row of running ostriches, another of dogs chasing gazelles or antelopes, and a third with figures of male and female ibexes. The style of the last row recalls the Scythian animal-style. Sixth century B.C. *Hermitage.* (viii, 571.)

[Rostovtzeff, *Iranians and Greeks*, Pl. VII, 1; Ebert, *Reall. d. Vorg.* VI, Pl. 81 *b*]

[b] GOLD FISH, probably a horse-trapping or armour plate, of Ionian workmanship. Found in Germany in Brandenburg near *Vettersfelde* and forming part of a treasure which belonged originally to a Scythian chieftain or part of the furniture of a Scythian grave. The body of the fish is decorated with two rows of figures: lions attacking hoofed animals and fishes, headed by a Triton; the tail bears a figure of an eagle; all in repoussé work. The extremities of the tail end in ram-heads. Early fifth century B.C. *Antiquarium, Berlin.* (viii, 571, 587.)

[A. Furtwängler, *Der Goldfund von Vettersfelde*, im 73 *Berliner Winckelmanns-programm* 1883 (reprinted in Furtwängler, *Kleine Schriften*, II (1912); Ebert, *Reall. der Vorg.* XIV, pp. 156 *sqq.*, Pl. 44]

[a]

GOLD CUP

[b]

GOLD FISH

[*a*] GOLD EARRINGS of Greek workmanship. Found in a grave of the necropolis of *Theodosia* in the Crimea. Fourth century B.C. *Hermitage.* (viii, 585.)

[Minns, *Scythians and Greeks*, p. 401, fig. 294, 3; Rostovtzeff, *Iranians and Greeks*, Pl. XVIII, 1]

[*b*] GOLD NECKLACE of Greek workmanship. Found in a grave of the necropolis of *Nymphaeum* (El-Tegen) in the Crimea. Fifth century B.C. *Ashmolean Museum, Oxford.* (viii, 585.)

[Rostovtzeff, *Iranians and Greeks*, Pl. XVI, 4]

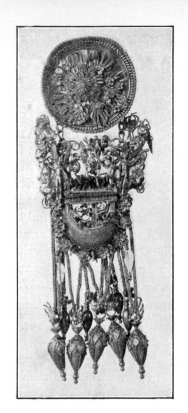

[a]

[b]

GOLD JEWELLERY

[*a*], [*b*] HANDLE and SHEATH of a SHORT SCYTHIAN SWORD (*akinakes*). Plated with gold, made by an Ionian artist for a Scythian customer or by a Scythian artisan trained by an Ionian. Found in a Scythian barrow-grave near the farm *Shumeiko, Romny, Poltava*. The handle is adorned with geometric ornaments in granulate work, like Ionian works of the same kind, and the sheath with figures of animals treated both in the Near Eastern and in the Scythian manner. The two heraldic ibexes above are orientalizing; the vertical row of seven cat-like creatures is Scythian in style. Sixth century B.C. In the *Museum, Kiev.* (viii, 571, 587.)

[Rostovtzeff, *Iranians and Greeks*, Pl. VIII, 3; W. Ginters, *Das Schwert der Skythen und der Sarmaten*, Pl. 3 c and 69 b (reconstruction of this and contemporary and related Scythian swords), cf. Ebert, *Reall. d. Vorg.* xiv, pp. 156 *sqq.*, Pl. 15]

[*c*] SHORT SCYTHIAN BRONZE SWORD (*akinakes*), probably of local Scythian workmanship. Found in a Scythian barrow near *Poltava*. The handle is adorned with cast figures of animals treated in the manner of the Scythian animal style (two feline and two hoofed animals, probably female elks or reindeer). Sixth century B.C. *Museum, Poltava.* Unpublished. (viii, 571, 587.)

[*d*] GOLD-PLATED SHEATH of a SCYTHIAN SWORD, probably of Panticapaean workmanship. Adorned with a running design in the Ionian animal style. The work is repoussé (lions and heads of a stag or reindeer), with the exception of the chape which bears the figure of a stylized mask or Medusa-head. Found in the side-grave of the barrow of *Solokha* (left side of the lower Dnieper). Fourth century B.C. *Hermitage.* (viii, 571, 587.)

[W. Ginters, *Das Schwert der Skythen und der Sarmaten*, Pl. 22 b; Ebert, *Reall. d. Vorg.* xii, pp. 294 *sqq.*, Pl. 81 b]

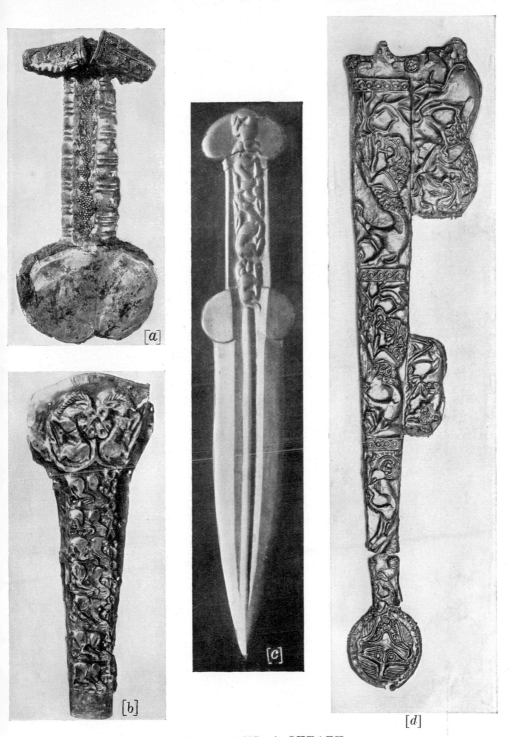

SWORDS AND A SHEATH

[a] Gold figure of a WILD BEAST (lioness?). Probably a decoration for armour. Scythian or Central Asiatic workmanship. Note in it traits which link this peculiar treatment of metal by the artist (the so-called *Schrägschnitt* or a peculiar kind of chip-carving) with the typical treatment of wood or bone; cp. 112 [b], [c]. Found in a barrow-grave near *Kelermes* in the Kuban region (cp. 78 and 80 [a]). The ears of the beast are inlaid with amber, the eye and the nostrils with enamel in proto-cloisonné technique. The paws of the animal, rendered in repoussé work, are shaped as cats curled up. The tail consists of six such medallions likewise in repoussé work. This treatment of extremities is one of the peculiarities of the Central Asiatic beast-style. Sixth century B.C. *Hermitage.* (viii, 571, 587.)

[Rostovtzeff, *Iranians and Greeks*, Pl. IX, 1; *idem, The Animal Style in S. Russia and China*, Pl. V, 2; Ebert, *Reall. d. Vorg.* XIII, Pl. 27 A (c); Borovka, *Scythian Art*, Pl. 12]

[b] Figure of an ANIMAL of FELINE species. Cast bronze, plated with gold. Scythian workmanship. Found in the grave of the *Zolotoj Kurgan* (Golden Barrow) near *Simferopol* in the Crimea. The gold sheath which covers the centre of the body of the beast is adorned with almond-shaped wire frames originally filled with enamel. Sixth century B.C. *Hermitage.* (viii, 571, 587.)

[Ebert, *Reall. d. Vorg.* XIII, Pl. 31 A (c); Borovka, *Scythian Art*, Pl. 13]

[c] Figure of an ANIMAL of FELINE species. Cast bronze, plated with gold. Scythian workmanship. Place of origin unknown. The shoulder of the beast is adorned with a stylized eagle, or eagle-griffin, head, which is a peculiarity of the Central Asiatic animal style (cp. 112 [b]). Sixth to fifth century B.C. *Louvre*, Department of Far Eastern Art. Unpublished.

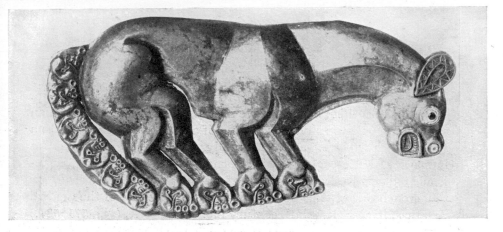

[a]

[b]

[c]

FANTASTIC ANIMALS

[a] BRONZE POLE-TOP. Cast bronze. Scythian workmanship. Found in a Scythian barrow-grave near the *Ulski Aul* in the Kuban region. The pole-top shows the shape of an eagle-head re duced to a stylized beak (spiral) and an equally stylized eye (formed as a human eye). The eagle-head is adorned with other stylized eagle-heads reduced to beaks and eyes of varying sizes. Below, a figure of a crouched ibex. The pole-top is a typical product of the Central Asiatic animal-style. Sixth century B.C. *Hermitage.* (viii, 571, 587.)

[Rostovtzeff, *Iranians and Greeks*, Pl. X A; *idem, Animal Style*, Pl. VI, 1, 2; Borovka, *Scythian Art*, Pls. 24 and 25; Ebert, *Reall. d. Vorg.* Pl. VI, 1, 2. Cf. Rostowzew, *Skythien und der Bosporus*, p. 264]

[b] BRONZE POLE-TOP. Cast bronze. Scythian workmanship. Place of origin unknown. Shape of a mule-head. Sixth to fifth century B.C. *Louvre, Paris.* Cp. Rostovtzeff, *Iranians and Greeks*, Pl. X C; Borovka, *Scythian Art*, Pl. 26 (almost identical pole-top from Kelermes, Kuban region). (viii, 571, 587.)

[c] BRONZE PLAQUE from horse-trappings. Cast bronze. Scythian workmanship. Found in one of the graves of the *Seven Brothers Barrows* in the Kuban region. Stylized female elk-head. Fifth century B.C. *Hermitage.* (viii, 571, 587.)

[Rostovtzeff, *Iranians and Greeks*, p. 196, fig. 22 c: *Animal Style*, Pl. X, 7; similar plaques, Borovka, *Scythian Art*, Pl. 5]

[d] BRONZE PLAQUE from horse-trappings. Cast bronze. Scythian workmanship. Found in one of the graves of the *Seven Brothers Barrows.* Stylized boar's head. Fifth century B.C. *Hermitage.*

[Minns, *Scythians and Greeks*, p. 214, fig. 115; Rostovtzeff, *Animal Style*, Pl. X, 8; Borovka, *Scythian Art*, Pl. 170]

[a]   [b]

POLE-TOPS

[c]

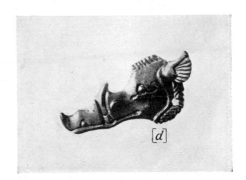

[d]

PLAQUES

BOSPORUS

[a] SILVER RHYTON. Persian or Graeco-Persian workmanship. Found in one of the graves of the *Seven Brothers Barrows* in the Kuban region. The end of the rhyton is shaped as the forepart of a winged ibex (an animal typical of Persian art). Fifth century B.C. *Hermitage.* (viii, 571, 587.)

[Minns, *Scythians and Greeks*, p. 211, fig. 110; Rostovtzeff, *Iranians and Greeks*, Pl. XII A; Ebert, *Reall. d. Vorg.* XII, pp. 84 *sqq.*, Pl. 18 A]

[b] GOLD ARMLET. Greek or Graeco-Persian workmanship. Found in one of the graves of the *Seven Brothers Barrows.* The body of the armlet consists of two fine flexible chains; the ends terminate in snakes' heads. Fifth to fourth century B.C. *Hermitage.* (viii, 571, 587.)

[Rostovtzeff, *Iranians and Greeks*, Pl. XV, 1]

[c], [d] GOLD PLAQUES of roughly triangular form. Originally probably nailed to the rim of a wooden or horn rhyton. Persian, or Graeco-Persian, workmanship. Found in one of the graves of the *Seven Brothers Barrows.* One of the plaques is adorned with a figure of a winged panther or tiger killing an ibex, the other with that of an eagle killing a kid. Fifth century B.C. *Hermitage.* (viii, 571, 587.)

[Minns, *Scythians and Greeks*, p. 211, fig. 112; Rostovtzeff, *Iranians and Greeks*, Pl. XIII; Ebert, *Reall. d. Vorg.* XII, p. 87, Pl. 19]

[e] GOLD PLAQUE, probably nailed originally to the rim of a wooden or horn rhyton, produced in one of the Greek cities of the Black Sea. Found probably in a Scythian barrow near *Maïkop* in the Kuban region. Sea-eagle carrying a sturgeon. Cp. the coins of Sinope and Olbia. Fifth century B.C. *Antiquarium, Berlin.* Unpublished. (viii, 587.)

[Cf. Rostowzew, *Skythien und der Bosporus*, p. 346]

[f] ENGRAVED GEM, enlarged. Persian or Graeco-Persian workmanship. Found in a barrow of the necropolis of *Nymphaeum* (El-Tegen) near Panticapaeum. Horned Persian lion-griffin. Fifth century B.C. *Ashmolean Museum, Oxford.* (viii, 571, 587.)

[Rostovtzeff, *Iranians and Greeks*, Pl. XVI, 1]

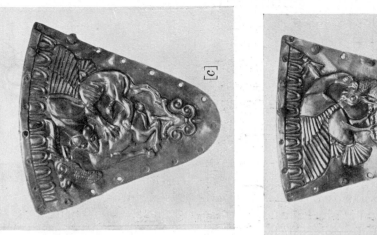

[c]

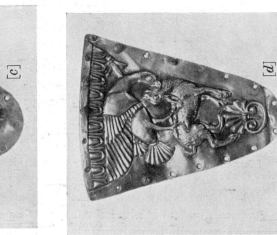

[d]

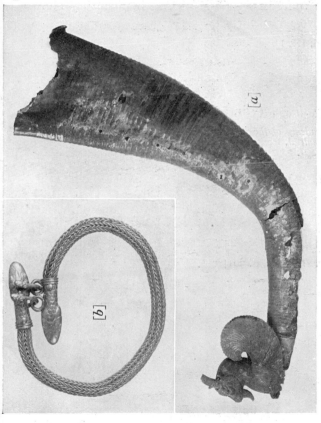

[a]

[b]

[f]

[e]

GRAECO-PERSIAN ART

[a] BRONZE PATERA HANDLE of Greek workmanship. Found in one of the graves of the *Seven Brothers Barrows* in the Kuban region. A Hermes Kriophoros of ornamental character. Sixth to fifth century B.C. *Hermitage.* (viii, 563.)

[*Compte-rendu de la Comm. Arch.* 1877, Atlas, I, 9; Minns, *Scythians and Greeks*, p. 378]

[b], [c] GOLD PLAQUES, originally sewn on to garments, of Panticapaean workmanship made for Scythian customers. Probably part of the same find to which belongs the plaque 90 [e]. Some plaques have the shape of stags with stylized horns, the extremities of which end in eagle-heads, some that of eagle-griffins. Fifth century B.C. *Metropolitan Museum, New York.* (viii, 587.)

[Rostovtzeff, *Animal Style*, Pl. IX, 1]

[d] BRONZE STAG. Handle of a Scythian kettle. Greek workmanship. Found in a barrow of the *Ulski Aul* in the Kuban region. Sixth century B.C. *Hermitage.* (viii, 563.)

[Borovka, *Bulletin of the Academy of the History of Material Civilization*, II, 1922, pp. 193 *sqq.*, Pl. II; Ebert, *Reall. d. Vorg.* XIV, p. 2, Pl. 1 C]

[e] BRONZE MIRROR with wooden handle. Greek workmanship. Found in one of the graves of the *Seven Brothers Barrows*. The lower part of the surface of the mirror is adorned with an engraved palmette. Another engraved design, added probably later by a Scythian artisan, shows two wild beasts attacking a deer. (viii, 563.)

[Rostowzew, *Skythien und der Bosporus*, p. 301]

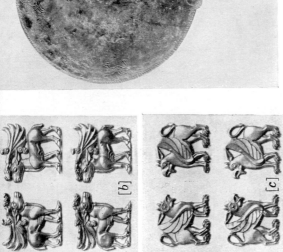

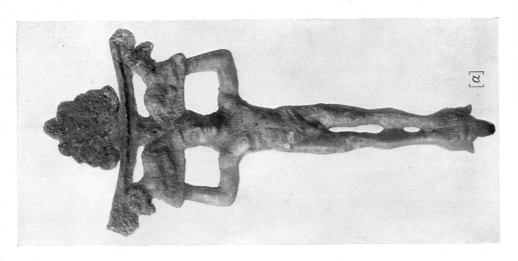

GREEK BRONZES AND SCYTHIAN GOLD PLAQUES

Two views of the TSARSKI KURGAN ('Royal' Barrow) near Kerch. First half of fourth century B.C.

[a] The interior, seen through the doorway. The courses up to the one numbered 7 are perpendicular, above that corbelled.

[b] The twelve courses of the vaults, corbelled out one above the other. (viii, 585).

[Reproduced from *Jahreshefte des oesterreichischen archaeologischen Instituts*, x, 1907, p. 236 *sq*. See Minns, *Scythians and Greeks*, p. 194]

[a]

[b]

THE 'ROYAL' BARROW

[a], [b] PAINTED CLAY VASES of Greek, probably Athenian, work-manship; found in a Greek grave of the necropolis of *Phanagoreia*. [a] Birth of Aphrodite; [b] winged Sphinx. Late fifth century B.C. *Hermitage*. (viii, 585.)

[Minns, *Scythians and Greeks*, p. 345, fig. 251; p. 344, fig. 250; Rostovtzeff, *Iranians and Greeks*, Pl. XVII, 1; Pridik, *Zeitschrift für bildende Kunst*, 18, pp. 172 *sqq.*; Phar-makowski, *Three polychrome vases in the form of statuettes found in Phanagoreia*, Memoirs of the Academy of the History of Mat. Civ. I, 1921; Rostowzew, *Skythien und der Bosporus,* p. 225. Often discussed and reproduced in works on the history of Greek art. Bibliography in M. H. Swindler, *Ancient Painting*, p. 462]

[a]

[b]

GREEK VASES

ARYBALLUS OF XENOPHANTUS. Work of an Athenian artist, perhaps resident at Panticapaeum. Found in a Greek grave at *Panticapaeum*. The body of the vase is adorned with figures in relief and painting. The figures in relief are coloured white, red and blue, with gilt accessories; the end-figures are flat in red-figure technique. The scene represents Persians on a hunting expedition, their names being inscribed beside the figures. The animals hunted are partly real, partly fantastic. The vase bears the inscription: **ΞΕΝΟΦΑΝΤΟΣ ΕΠΟΙΗΣΕΝ ΑΘΗΝ.** Shortly before 400 B.C. *Hermitage.* (viii, 585.)

[*Compte-rendu de la Comm. Arch.* 1866, Atlas, Pl. IV; *Antiquités du Bosphore Cimmérien*, Pl. XLV (here reproduced); Minns, *Scythians and Greeks*, p. 343, fig. 249. Often discussed and reproduced. Bibliography in Pfuhl, *Malerei und Zeichnung der Griechen*, II, pp. 591 and 600; M. H. Swindler, *Ancient Painting*, p. 297]

ARYBALLUS OF XENOPHANTUS

[a] CLAY VASE painted with various colours in the distemper technique. Panticapaean workmanship. Found in a rock-cut grave of the necropolis of *Panticapaeum*. A Greek fighting an Amazon. Third century B.C. *Hermitage*. (viii, 585.)

[*Compte-rendu de la Comm. Arch.* 1878–9, Atlas, Pl. I, 5; Minns, *Scythians and Greeks*, p. 348, fig. 253; M. H. Swindler, *Ancient Painting*, fig. 565]

[b] CLAY AMPHORA with painted and plastic ornaments painted in various colours. Greek workmanship. Found at *Olbia*. Third century B.C. *Hermitage*. (viii, 585.)

Trever, *Materials for the Archaeology of S. Russia*, xxxv, 1918]

VASES

[a]

[b]

Frieze of a LARGE SILVER AMPHORA. Panticapaean workmanship. Found in one of the graves of the *Chertomlyk Barrow* on the right bank of the lower Dnieper. Scythians in the prairies of S. Russia lassoing and saddling horses on the eve of a military expedition. Fourth century B.C. *Hermitage.* (viii, 571, 587.)

[Reproduced from *Antike Denkmäler*, IV, Pl. 46. (F. Bruckmann, A.G.) To the bibliography given there by Waldhauer add P. Jacobsthal, *Ornamentik griechischer Vasen*, Pls. 142, 143]

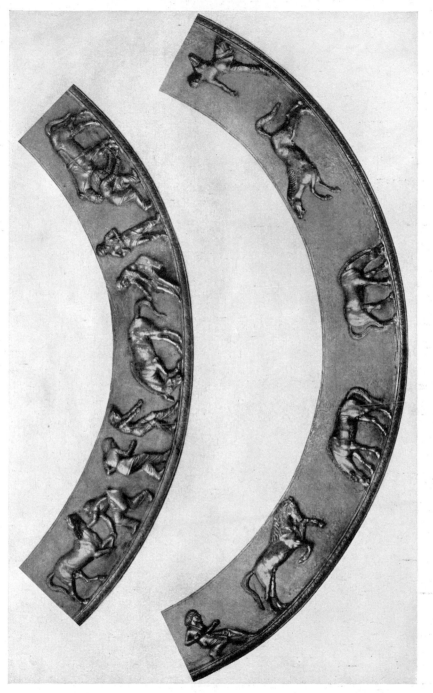

FRIEZE OF A SILVER AMPHORA

[a] GOLD PATERA. Panticapaean workmanship. Found in the side-grave of the *Solokha Barrow* on the left side of the lower Dnieper. The patera is adorned with figures in repoussé work: three rows of grouped animals showing wild beasts killing various creatures. Two Greek inscriptions probably give the name of the artist and that of the owner. Fourth century B.C. *Hermitage.* (viii, 571, 587.)

[Rostovtzeff, *Iranians and Greeks*, Pl. XX, 12; Ebert, *Reall. d. Vorg.* IV, Pl. 85; XII, p. 298, § 10]

[b] SILVER BOWL. Panticapaean workmanship. Found in the side-grave of the *Solokha Barrow*. Young Scythians on horseback hunting lions. Between them appear two lions playing with each other, and, on the opposite side, a group of two Molossian dogs. Fourth century B.C. *Hermitage.* (viii, 571, 587.)

[Rostovtzeff, *Iranians and Greeks*, Pl. XX, 12; Ebert, *Reall. d. Vorg.* XII, Pl. 83]

[a]

GOLD PATERA

[b]

SILVER BOWL

[a] GOLD PLAQUE sewn originally on to a belt. Local workmanship; found in a Scythian grave in a barrow near *Axjutinzy, Romny,* Poltava. A Scythian king, or chieftain, seated holding a battle-axe in his left hand and a drinking cup in his right. A bow-and-arrow case (*gorytos*) hangs on his right side. Repoussé work. Third century B.C. *Historical Museum, Moscow.* (viii, 571, 587.)

[Minns, *Scythians and Greeks*, p. 182, fig. 75 *bis*; Rostovtzeff, *Bull. de la Comm. Arch.* 49 (1913), p. 8, fig. 3; Ebert, *Reall. d. Vorg.* XIII, p. 95, Pl. 39 F (a)]

[b]–[n] GOLD PLAQUES originally sewn on garments. Panticapaean workmanship. Repoussé work. Found in various Scythian barrows of the steppes of S. Russia. [b]–[d] show ritual scenes: [b] 'sacramental draught' of a Scythian prince administered by the Great Goddess of the Scythians; [c] the Great Goddess and her sacred animals (dog and raven); [d] ritual wrestling. Plaques [g] and [j] recall contemporary Greek coin-types. The rest are purely ornamental. Some of the plaques belong to the fifth century B.C., the majority to the fourth, some to the third. *Hermitage* and *Museum, Kiev.* (viii, 571, 587.)

[Rostovtzeff, *Bull. de la Comm. Arch.* 49 (1913); *Iranians and Greeks*, Pl. XXIII; Minns, *Scythians and Greeks*, *passim*, esp. p. 208]

106

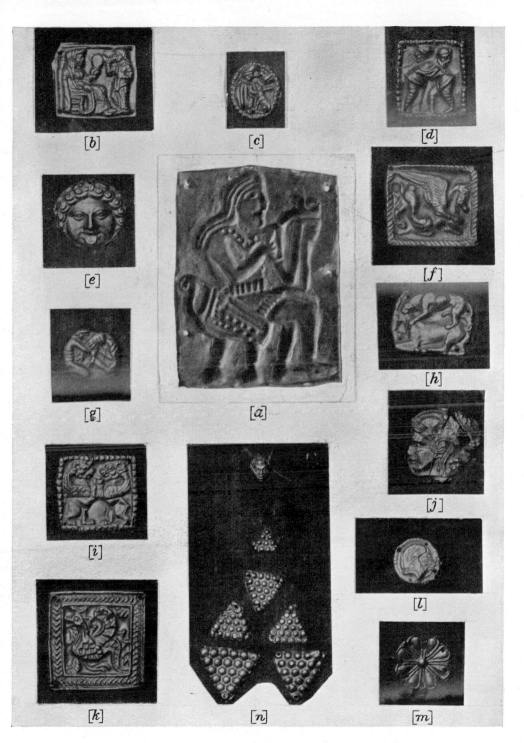

GOLD PLAQUES

[a]–[d] GOLD ORNAMENTS in open work. Probably ornaments for saddles. Scythian, or Graeco-Scythian, workmanship. Found partly in the earth, partly in the graves of the *Alexandropol Barrow* (Lugo-vaja Mogila) on right side of the lower Dnieper. Degenerate and geometricized Ionian and Scythian animal figures both single and in groups. Third century B.C. *Hermitage.* (viii, 587.)

[*Recueil d'antiquités de la Scythie*, Pl. XV; Minns, *Scythians and Greeks*, p. 155, fig. 42; Ebert, *Reall. d. Vorg.* XIII, pp. 87 *sqq.*, Pls. 36 A and 36 C]

[e] BRONZE POLE-TOP. Scythian workmanship in cast bronze. Found in the earth of the *Alexandropol Barrow.* Winged figure of the Great Goddess of the Scythians. Third century B.C. *Hermitage.* (viii, 584.)

[*Recueil d'antiquités de la Scythie*, Pl. I, 8; Minns, *Scythians and Greeks*, p. 154, fig. 40; Ebert, *Reall. d. Vorg.* XIII, Pl. 35 D (c)]

[f] IRON OPEN-WORK FIGURE, nailed originally on to a funeral chariot or on to a funeral canopy, plated with gold. Found in the earth of the *Alexandropol Barrow.* Figure of the winged Great Goddess of the Scythians, the πότνια θηρῶν, holding two stags. Third century B.C. *Hermitage.* (viii, 584.)

[*Recueil d'antiquités de la Scythie*, Pl. I, 3, 4; Ebert, *Reall. d. Vorg.* XIII, Pl. 35 D (g)]

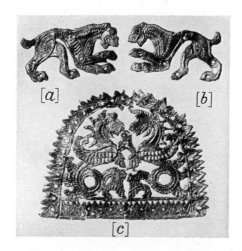

GOLD ORNAMENTS

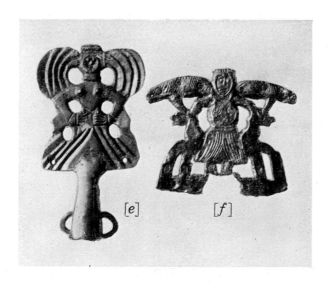

FIGURES OF THE WINGED GODDESS

Eight GOLD CIRCULAR PLAQUES (phalerae) from horse-trappings.
Repoussé work. Indo-Hellenic workmanship (?). Found in a horse's
grave of the *Alexandropol Barrow* on the lower Dnieper. [*a*] Single
figures of animals (eagle, winged horse, bull and lion): [*b*] bulls'
heads forming a solar wheel around a human face in front view,
four boars' heads forming a solar wheel around a rosette, and a
rosette of eight leaves; all probably symbols of a solar religion
(cf. p. 76 above). Third century B.C. *Hermitage.* (viii, 588.)

[*Recueil d'antiquités de la Scythie*, Pl. VII, 1, 3, 7, 6; Rostovtzeff, *Recueil Kondakoff*,
Pl. XXII; Ebert, *Reall. d. Vorg.* XIII, Pl. 36 C (*c*)–(*k*)]

[a]

[b]

GOLD PLAQUES

[*a*] GOLD PLAQUE nailed originally to the rim of a wooden or horn rhyton. Persian, or Graeco-Persian, workmanship. Repoussé work. Found in one of the graves of the *Seven Brothers Barrows*. Figure of a wolf-headed dragon with Asiatic wings and a tail ending in the head of a goose. Fifth century B.C. *Hermitage*. (viii, 571, 587.)

[Minns, *Scythians and Greeks*, p. 211, fig. 111; Rostovtzeff, *Iranians and Greeks*, Pl. XIII D; Ebert, *Reall. d. Vorg.* xiii, Pl. 19 D; Borovka, *Scythian Art*, Pl. 20 A]

[*b*] GOLD STAG, probably a decoration for armour, or a horse-trapping, and gold chain adorned with gold cylinders surmounted by figurines of lions. Scythian or Central-Asiatic workmanship. The stag in repoussé work has the eye and ear inlaid with enamel. Under the stylized horns is an eagle's head. Found in Hungary near *Zöldhalompuszta* in a cremation grave. Sixth century B.C. (viii, 571, 573.)

[N. Fettich, *La Trouvaille scythe de Zöldhalompuszta près de Miskolc, Hongrie*, in *Archaeologia Hungarica*, iii, 1928, pp. 37 *sqq.*; G. Childe, *The Danube in Prehistory*, 1929, pp. 394 *sqq.*]

[*c*] GOLD STAG, probably a decoration for armour or a horse-trapping. Scythian or Central-Asiatic workmanship. Repoussé work. The eye and ear originally inlaid with enamel. Found in Hungary near *Tápios-Szent-Marten* in a cremation grave. (viii, 571, 573.)

[N. Fettich, *op. cit.*; G. Wilke, in Ebert, *Reall. d. Vorg.* xii, Pl. 66 *a*; Rostovtzeff, *Animal Style*, Pl. V, 1]

[a]

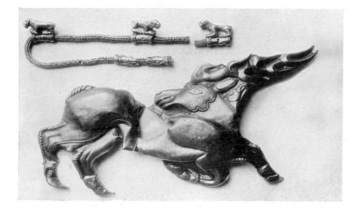

[b]

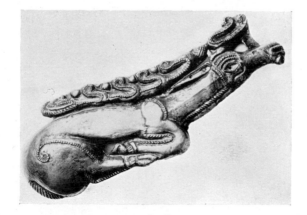

[c]

GOLD ORNAMENTS

MARBLE PORTRAIT HEAD, life size, perhaps of a Pergamene
prince from *Pergamum*. Now in *Berlin*. (viii, 600.)

[*Altertümer von Pergamon*, VII, Pl. XXIV]

8-2

(*a*) MARBLE PANOPLY found in *Rhodes*; in the *Museum of Rhodes*. (viii, 637.)

[*Clara Rhodos*, I, 1928]

(*b*) A ROCK-CARVING at *Lindus* in Rhodes representing the stern of a Rhodian ship. One of the rudders is lashed to the side; the helmsman's seat is upon the deck under the curved *aphlaston*. (viii, 638.)

[*Bulletin de l'Acádemie royale des Sciences et des Lettres* (Copenhagen), 1907, p. 31]

[a] RHODIAN MARBLE PANOPLY

[b] SHIP'S STERN AT LINDUS

[a] ARIADNE, from the southern slopes of the *Acropolis at Athens*; *National Museum, Athens*. About 300 B.C. (viii, 670.)

[*Phot. English Photographic Co.*]

[b] MENANDER, terminal bust from neighbourhood of *Naples*; in *Boston*. Roman copy probably of an original by the sons of Praxiteles, set up in the theatre of Dionysus at Athens in the early third century B.C. (viii, 671.)

[Delbrück, *Antike Porträts*, Pl. 20]

[c] THEMIS by Chaerestratus, from *Rhamnus*; *National Museum, Athens*. Late fourth or early third century B.C. (viii, 670.)

[*Phot. English Photographic Co.*]

[d] SELENE descending to Endymion. Found in *Rome*; in the *Vatican*. Roman copy from a Greek original of the early third century B.C. The arms, right foot and other patches are modern. (viii, 670.)

[*Phot. Brogi*]

[a] ARIADNE

[b] MENANDER

[c] THEMIS

[d] SELENE

[*a*] DIONYSUS, from the choragic monuments of Thrasyllus and Thrasycles, southern slope of Acropolis, *Athens*; in the *British Museum*. 320 or 271 B.C. (viii, 670.)

[*Phot. Prof. B. Ashmole*]

[*b*] DEMOSTHENES, probably from the neighbourhood of *Tusculum*; in the *Vatican*: Roman copy in marble from a bronze original by Polyeuctus, 280 B.C. The most serious restorations are the forearms, and the hands, which in the original were clasped. (viii, 671.)

[*Phot. Brogi*]

[*c*] NILE, from a temple of Isis in *Rome*; in the *Vatican*. Copy of the first century A.D. from an original of the third century B.C. Many details restored, especially parts of the children. (viii, 671.)

[*Phot. Brogi*]

[a] DIONYSUS

[b] DEMOSTHENES

[c] NILE

[a] Head of a girl, *Taranto*. Roman copy from an Athenian original of the early third century B.C. (viii, 671.)

[*Phot. Prof. B. Ashmole*]

[b] Head of a MUSE; in the *Lateran Museum, Rome*. Roman copy from an original of the third century B.C. (viii, 677.)

[*Phot. Alinari*]

[c] Head of POLYHYMNIA; in *Dresden*. Roman copy from an original of the third century B.C. (See p. 142 [c].) (viii, 677.)

[*Phot. Dresden Museum*]

[d] Head of a statue of TYCHE. (See p. 124 [d].) (viii, 124.)

[*Phot. Faraglia*]

[a]

[b]

[c]

[d]

FEMALE HEADS

[*a*], [*b*] Small bronzes of TYCHE in *Florence* and in the *de Clercq* Collection. The swimming river-god, Orontes, appears beside the second, but is missing from the first.

[*c*] TYCHE of Antioch. Roman copy in marble from the bronze original by Eutychides. From *Rome*: in *Budapest*.

[*Photographs F. Bruckmann A.G., Munich*]

[*d*] YOUNG TYCHE. Roman copy in marble after a bronze original by Eutychides, early third century B.C. From the *Esquiline*; *Palazzo dei Conservatori, Rome.* (Cf. p. 122 [*d*].) (viii, 674, 675.)

[*Phot. Alinari*]

[a]   [b]

[c]   [d]

FIGURES OF TYCHE

The statue of VICTORY from *Samothrace*; in the *Louvre*.

By a Rhodian sculptor, set up to commemorate the battle of Cos, *c.* 258 B.C. It recalls an earlier (lost) statue dedicated by Demetrius Poliorcetes, as a memorial of the battle of Salamis in Cyprus, which is reproduced on certain of his coins. (Cf. *Vol. of Plates*, ii, 10 [*k*].) (vii, 714 *sq.*; viii, 675.)

[*Phot. Giraudon*]

VICTORY FROM SAMOTHRACE

[*a*] LAOCOON and his sons attacked by serpents. From the *Palace of Titus, Rome*; in the *Vatican*. By Agesander, Polydorus and Athenodorus of Rhodes, early first century B.C. Photograph from a cast in which one of the boys and other parts have been removed. (viii, 678.)

[*Phot. University of Berlin*]

[*b*] The punishment of DIRCE by Zethus and Amphion. From the *Baths of Caracalla, Rome*; in *Naples*. Roman version in marble of the bronze by Apollonius and Tauriscus of Tralles. The men's heads, legs and arms, the woman's head and torso, and many other parts, are modern. (viii, 678.)

[*Phot. F. Bruckmann A.G., Munich*]

[b] DIRCE

[a] LAOCOON

[a], [b] Roman copies in marble from bronze originals of the late fourth century B.C. probably by Lysippus or his school. From *Herculaneum*; in *Dresden*. (viii, 677.)

[*Phot. Dresden Museum*]

[c] Figure from the balustrade of the altar of Athena Polias, *Priene*; in *Berlin*. Late fourth century B.C. (viii, 677.)

[*Phot. Berlin Museum*]

[d] Statue from *Magnesia*; in *Constantinople*. About 200 B.C. (viii, 677.)

[*Phot. Sebah and Joaillier*]

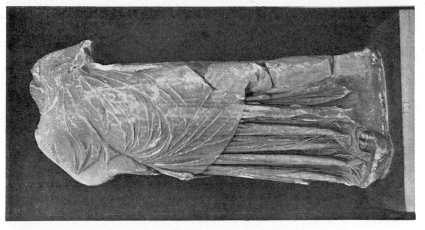

[d]

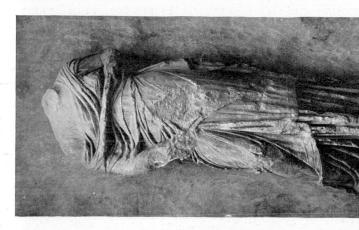

[c]

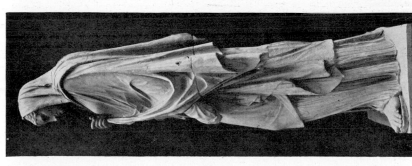

[b]

[a]

DRAPED FEMALE FIGURES

[*a*] HERMES resting while on a journey. Roman version in bronze of a bronze original of the third century B.C. Lysippic school. From *Herculaneum*; in *Naples*. (viii, 675.)

[*Phot. Anderson*]

[*b*] Boy praying. Bronze copy of a bronze original by Boedas, a pupil of Lysippus; early third century B.C. From *Italy*; in *Berlin*. (viii, 673.)

[*Phot. Berlin Museum*]

[*c*] Boy taking a thorn from his foot. Roman fountain-figure, a copy in marble after a bronze original of the third century B.C. From *Rome*; in the *British Museum*. (viii, 675.)

[*Phot. British Museum*]

132

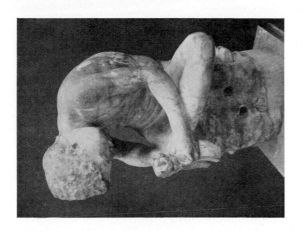

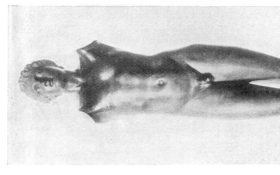

[a]

[b]

[c]

MALE FIGURES

[*a*] Head of a dying oriental—probably a Persian killed in a battle against Athenians. Copy, in marble of Asia Minor, from a bronze original of the dedication of Attalus I, third quarter of the third century B.C. From the *Palatine*; *Terme Museum, Rome.* (viii, 679.)

[*Phot. Anderson*]

[*b*] A Gaul stabbing himself to avoid capture, after killing his wife: the 'Ludovisi Gaul.' Copy, in marble of Asia Minor, from a bronze group forming part of the dedication of Attalus I at Pergamum, third quarter of the third century B.C. *Terme Museum, Rome.* The most serious restoration is the right arm of the man, the hand of which should be held with the thumb upward, so lowering the elbow. (viii, 679.)

[*Phot. Brogi*]

[a] DYING PERSIAN

[b] THE LUDOVISI GAUL

[a] MARSYAS tied to a tree to be flayed. Copy of an original of the first Pergamene School. From *Tarsus*; in *Constantinople*.

[*Phot. Sebah and Joaillier*]

[b] Scythian slave sharpening his knife before flaying Marsyas. Copy of an original of the first Pergamene school. *Uffizi, Florence*. The statue has suffered from patching and repolishing. (viii, 680.)

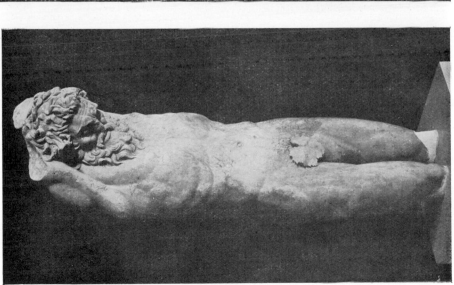

[a]

[b]

THE PUNISHMENT OF MARSYAS

[a] A fighting Gaul, from Delos; *National Museum, Athens*. An original of the end of the third century B.C. (viii, 681.)

[*Phot. Alinari*]

[b] A dead barbarian. Copy in marble from a bronze original set up on the Acropolis at Athens at the end of the third century B.C. by Attalus I. *Palace of the Doges, Venice*. (viii, 681.)

[*Phot. Giraudon*]

[c] MENELAUS carrying the body of PATROCLUS. Copy from an original of the late third century B.C. *Loggia de' Lanzi, Florence*. The head, arms, and upper part of the body of Menelaus, and the arms of Patroclus, as well as other parts, are modern. (viii, 682.)

[*Phot. Seemann, Leipzig*]

[c]

MENELAUS

[a]

[b]

GAULS

[*a*], [*c*] Young satyr fighting a snake-legged giant. From *Rome*; *Palazzo dei Conservatori*. Copy of a Pergamene original of the late third century B.C. (viii, 683.)

[Stuart Jones, *Conservatori Catal.* Pl. 28]

[*b*] Head of a young satyr repulsed by a nymph. From *Tivoli*; in the *British Museum*. Copy of an original of the early second century B.C. (viii, 683.)

[*d*] Head of an hermaphrodite escaping from an old satyr. From the neighbourhood of *Rome*; *Ince Blundell Hall, Lancashire*. Copy of an original of the early second century B.C. (viii, 683.)

[*e*] Head of the goddess NIGHT from the Great Altar of *Pergamum*; *Berlin*. From a cast. First half of second century B.C. (viii, 687.)

[*Phots. Prof. B. Ashmole*]

[a]

[b]　[c]

SATYRS

[d]　[e]

HERMAPHRODITE　'NIGHT'

[*a*] Bronze statuette of a satyr, from *Pompeii*; in the *Naples Museum*. Copy from an original of the late third century B.C. (viii, 682.)

[*Phot. Anderson*]

[*b*] Satyr turning to look at his tail. From *Rome*; *Terme Museum*. Copy from a bronze original of the late third century B.C. Parts of the legs are modern: the head is a cast from another replica. (viii, 677.)

[*Phot. Anderson*]

[*c*] Statue of POLYHYMNIA, the muse of lyric poetry. Copy from an original of the late third century B.C. (See also p. 122 [*c*].) Photograph from a cast combining a body in Berlin with a head in Dresden. (viii, 677.)

[Rodenwaldt, *Die Kunst der Antike*, p. 452]

[a] SATYR

[b] SATYR

[c] POLYHYMNIA

[a] APHRODITE at the bath. From *Vienne*; in the *Louvre*. Roman copy from an original by Doedalsas of Bithynia, about 200 B.C. (viii, 684.)

[*Phot. Alinari*]

[b] An old woman with an empty wine-jar. Copy in marble from a bronze original by Myron of Thebes set up at Smyrna about 200 B.C. From *Italy*; in *Munich*; *Glyptothek*. The nose, right arm, left shoulder and breast, left foot and other patches are modern. (viii, 685.)

[*Phot. Munich Glyptothek*]

[c] Boy struggling with a goose. Copy in marble from a bronze original by Boëthus of Chalcedon, early second century B.C. From *Rome*; in *Munich*; *Glyptothek*. Some small patches on the child's face, and the head of the goose, are modern. Photograph from a cast. (viii, 684.)

[c] BOY AND GOOSE

[b] OLD WOMAN

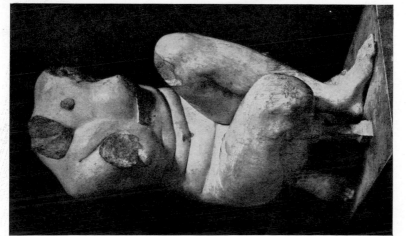

[a] APHRODITE

[*a*], [*b*] ERos sleeping. From *Rome*; *Palazzo dei Conservatori*. Copy from an original perhaps by Polycles of Athens, about 200 B.C. (viii, 684.)

[*Phots.* [*a*] *Prof. B. Ashmole*, [*b*] *Faraglia*]

[*c*], [*d*] Hermaphrodite sleeping. From *Rome*; *Terme Museum*. Copy from a bronze, perhaps by Polycles of Athens, about 200 B.C. (viii, 684.)

[*Phot. Brogi*]

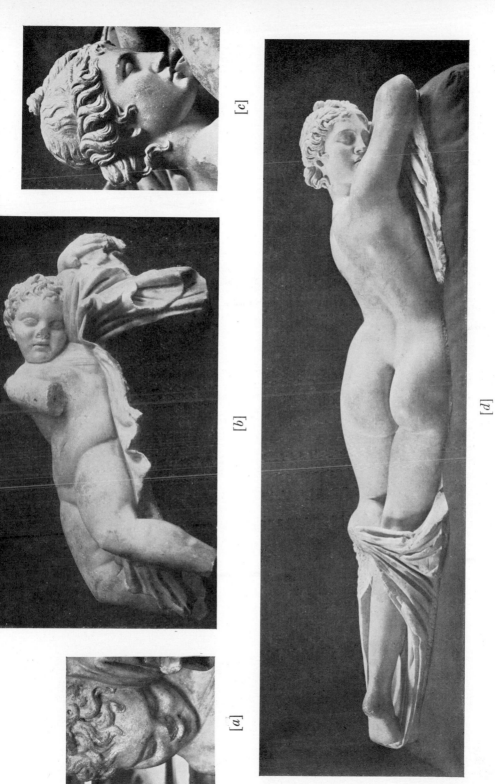

[c]

[b]

[a]

[d]

SLEEPING·FIGURES

ATHENA, crowned by Victory, tears Alcyoneus from the earth to destroy him. Ge rises to beg mercy for her sons. From the frieze of the Great Altar of *Pergamum*; in *Berlin*. Early second century B.C. (See p. 188 [*a*].) (viii, 686.)

[*Phot. Giraudon*, from a cast]

PART OF THE MAIN FRIEZE OF THE GREAT ALTAR OF PERGAMUM

[a] The legend of Telephus: the building of the boat for Auge. From the internal frieze of the Great Altar at *Pergamum;* in *Berlin.* Second quarter of the second century B.C. (viii, 687.)

[*Phot. Berlin Museum*]

[b] Worshippers approaching a god and goddess. Said to have come from *Corinth;* in *Munich; Glyptothek.* Athenian work of the third century B.C. (viii, 688.)

[*Phot. Munich Glyptothek*]

[a]

[b]

RELIEFS

[a], [b] Head of CHIRON the centaur, part of a group showing the musical education of Achilles. From the *Esquiline, Rome*; *Palazzo dei Conservatori*. Most of the nose is modern. Copy from an original of the first half of the second century B.C. (viii, 685.)

[*Phots.* [a] *Prof. B. Ashmole,* [b] *Alinari*]

[c] PAN teaching OLYMPUS or DAPHNIS to play the pipe; *Naples Museum*. Copy of the second century A.D. from an original of the first half of the second century B.C. The hands, and other patches, are modern. (viii, 685.)

[*Phot. Alinari*]

[a]   [b]

CHIRON

[c] PAN AND OLYMPUS

[a] Head of a woman, from *Pergamum*; in *Berlin*. Second Pergamene School. (viii, 687.)

[*Phot. Berlin Museum*]

[b] Head of the statue of APHRODITE from *Melos*; in the *Louvre*. (See p. 156 [c].) (viii, 691.)

[c] Colossal head of a goddess, by Damophon of Messene; in the *Capitoline Museum, Rome*. Mid second century B.C. (viii, 690.)

[*Phot. Alinari*]

[d] Head of ATHENA by Eubulides of Athens; *National Museum, Athens*. Second half of second century B.C. (viii, 692.)

[*Phot. English Photographic Co.*]

[a]

[b]

[c]

[d]

FEMALE HEADS

[a] Statue from *Pergamum*; in *Berlin*. Second Pergamene School, first half of second century B.C. (viii, 687.)

[*Pergamon, Plates, VII*, Pl. XIV]

[b] APHRODITE from *Capua*; in *Naples*. Roman copy in marble after a bronze original of the later fourth century B.C.

(*Note:* Against the view stated in the text (viii, 691) that this is a copy of the statue of Aphrodite on the Acropolis of Corinth, see O. Broneer in *Univ. of California Publications in Archaeology*, i, no. 2, pp. 65 *sqq.*)

[c] APHRODITE from *Melos*; in the *Louvre*. By ...andros, of Antioch on the Maeander, mid second century B.C. (Cf. p. 154 [b].) (viii, 691.)

[a]

FIGURE FROM PERGAMUM

[b]

APHRODITE FROM CAPUA

[c] APHRODITE FROM MELOS

[a] Warrior, by Agasias of Ephesus, end of the second century B.C. From *Anzio*; in the *Louvre*. (viii, 691.)

[*Phot. University of Berlin*, from a cast]

[b] Boxer resting. Bronze statue signed on the left glove by Apollonius son of Nestor, an Athenian, first century B.C. From the *Tiber*; in the *Terme Museum*. The rock is modern. (viii, 693.)

[*Phot. Alinari*]

[b] BOXER

[a] WARRIOR

[*a*] Satyr and nymphs. Archaistic relief, first century A.D. In *Rome, Palazzo dei Conservatori.* (viii, 692.)

[*Phot. Alinari*]

[*b*] Relief on one side of a four-sided marble basis or altar from *Capri*; in the *British Museum.* Early first century A.D. (viii, 692.)

[*Phot. British Museum*]

[*c*] Boy, by Stephanus, pupil of Pasiteles; from *Rome,* in the *Villa Albani.* End of the first century B.C. The right arm, half of the left forearm with the hand, and other parts are modern. (viii, **693.**)

[*d*] Group, perhaps Electra recognizing Orestes; by Menelaus, pupil of Stephanus, in the *Terme Museum, Rome.* First half of the first century A.D. (viii, **694.**)

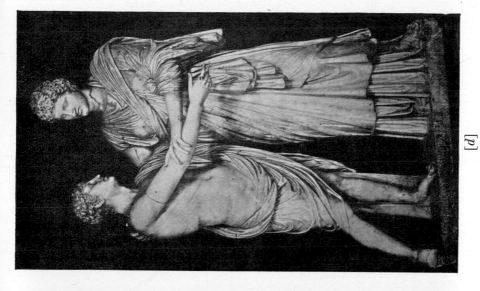

[d]

GROUP, BY MENELAUS

[c]

BOY, BY STEPHANUS

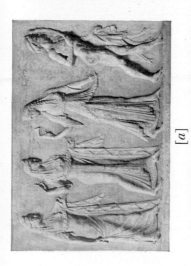

[a]

[b]

RELIEFS

[*a*] EPICURUS. Roman copy in marble from an original of the first half of the third century B.C. In the *Capitoline Museum, Rome.*

[*Phot. Oxford University Press*]

[*b*] A Greek poet, perhaps Epicharmus or Philemon. Roman copy in bronze from an original of the second century B.C. From *Herculaneum*; in *Naples.*

[*Phot. Anderson*]

[*c*], [*d*] CN. POMPEIUS MAGNUS. Third quarter of first century B.C. *Glyptotek Ny Carlsberg, Copenhagen.* (viii, 694.)

[*Phot. Ny Carlsberg Glyptotek*]

[a] EPICURUS

[b] A POET

[c]

[d]

[c], [d] CN. POMPEIUS MAGNUS

[a] Head of *Alexander the Great*, diademed and with the ram's horn of Ammon in his hair, from a coin of Lysimachus. 323–281 B.C.

[b] *Demetrius Poliorcetes*, diademed and with a bull's horn in his hair. 306–283 B.C.

[c] *Antiochus I*, diademed. 293–261 B.C.

[d] *Philetaerus* (284–263 B.C.), wreathed and diademed on a coin of *Eumenes II* of *Pergamum*. 197–159 B.C.

[e] *Berenice II*, wife of *Ptolemy Euergetes*, a gold octodrachm minted in *Ephesus*. The queen with diademed and veiled head. 258–222 B.C.

[f] *Antiochus III the Great*. 223–187 B.C.

[g] *Mithridates II*, King of *Pontus*. c. 255–220 B.C.

[h] *Euthydemus I*, King of *Bactria*. c. 222–187 B.C.

[i] *Euthydemus II*, King of *Bactria*, probably grandson of the last.

[j] *Antimachus I*, King of *Bactria*. Second century B.C.

[k] *Orophernes*, pretender to the throne of *Cappadocia*, a coin minted at *Priene*. 158–157 B.C.

[l] *Mithridates VI, the Great, King of Pontus*. 120–63 B.C.

[m] *Cleopatra VII*, 51–30 B.C.

All, except [e] gold, and [m] bronze, are silver tetradrachms, and all are slightly enlarged. The coins are in the *British Museum*. (viii,694.)

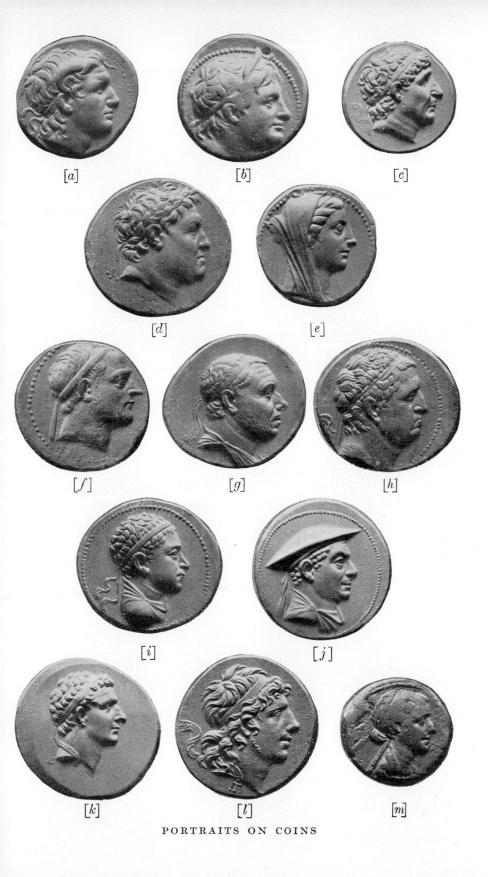

[a]   [b]   [c]

[d]   [e]

[f]   [g]   [h]

[i]   [j]

[k]   [l]   [m]

PORTRAITS ON COINS

ACHILLES, hidden among the daughters of Lycomedes, is discovered by Odysseus and Diomed. Copy of the first century A.D., from a painting of the third century B.C. From *Pompeii*; in *Naples*. (viii, 695.)

[*Phot. F. Bruckmann A.G., Munich*]

ACHILLES IN SCYROS

Wall painting of the first century B.C. after an original of the late third century B.C. from *Boscoreale, near Pompeii,* in the *Metropolitan Museum, New York.* [*a*] A Macedonian king and a sibyl (?). [*b*] A king and his queen (?). (viii, 696.)

[Barnabei, *Villa di P. Fannio Sinistore*, Pls. VI, VIII]

168

[a]

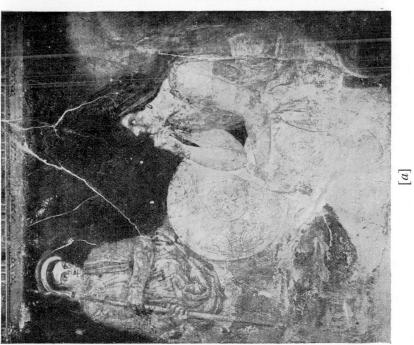

[b]

PAINTINGS FROM BOSCOREALE

HERACLES in bondage to OMPHALE in Lydia. Copy, of the first
century B.C. or A.D., from a picture by an artist of Asia Minor of
the third century B.C. From *Pompeii*; in *Naples*. (viii, 696.)

[*Phot. Sommer*]

HERACLES AND OMPHALE

HERACLES finds his son TELEPHUS in Arcadia. Copy, of the first century A.D., from a Pergamene painting of the second century B.C. From *Herculaneum*; in *Naples*. (viii, 697.)

HERACLES FINDING TELEPHUS

The initiation of a bride in Dionysiac ritual; after a painting of the second century B.C. *Villa Item, Pompeii.* (viii, 697.)

[*Phot. Alinari*]

PAINTING IN THE VILLA ITEM

[*a*] MEDEA contemplating the murder of her children. A copy of the first century A.D., probably after Timomachus of Byzantium, early first century B.C. From *Herculaneum*; in *Naples*. (viii, 698).

[*Phot. Alinari*]

[*b*] ORESTES and PYLADES before the temple of Artemis in Tauris. A copy, of the first century A.D., probably after Timomachus. From *Pompeii*; in *Naples*. (viii, 699.)

[*Phot. Sommer*]

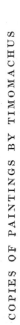

[a]

[b]

COPIES OF PAINTINGS BY TIMOMACHUS

[a] Visit to a wise woman. Mosaic by Dioscurides of Samos after a picture of the second century B.C. From *Pompeii*; in *Naples*. (viii, 699.)

[*Phot. Alinari*]

[b] Still life. Graeco-Roman painting of the first century B.C. From *Pompeii*; in *Naples*. (viii, 700.)

[*Phot. F. Bruckmann A.G., Munich*]

[b]

STILL LIFE

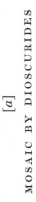

[a]

MOSAIC BY DIOSCURIDES

Landscapes from the Odyssey, found on the *Esquiline*; in the *Vatican*. [*a*] The Laestrygones destroying the ships of Odysseus. [*b*] Circe's island. From a Graeco-Roman frieze of the first century B.C. (viii, 700.)

[*Phot. F. Bruckmann A.G., Munich*]

[a]   [b]

LANDSCAPES FROM THE ODYSSEY

[*a*] Magnesian entablature. In *Berlin*. (viii, 701.)
[*Magnesia*, Blatt V]

[*b*] 'Hall of the Bulls.' In *Delos*. Detail and section. (viii, 702.)
[*Bulletin de Correspondance Hellénique*, VIII, 1884]

[*c*] *Miletus*; elevation of the Bouleuterion, restored. (viii, 703.)
[*Milet*, I, 2, Pl. VI]

[a] MAGNESIA

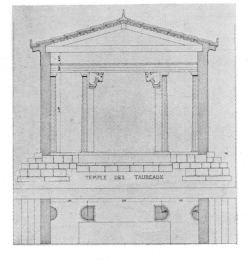

[b] DELOS

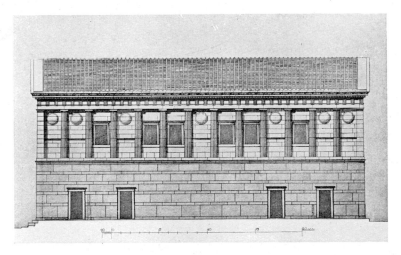

[c] MILETUS

Perspective view of the Acropolis of *Pergamum*, actual state. (viii, 705.)

[Collignon, *Pergame*, Pl. III]

TEMPLE OF TRAJAN
IONIC TEMPLE

SANCTUARY OF ATHENA   ALTAR OF ZEUS
THEATRE   TERRACE   TEMPLE OF DIONYSUS

THE ACROPOLIS OF PERGAMUM (*Bird's-Eye View*)

Restored plan of *Pergamum*. (viii, 705.)

[Collignon, *Pergame*, Pl. XI]

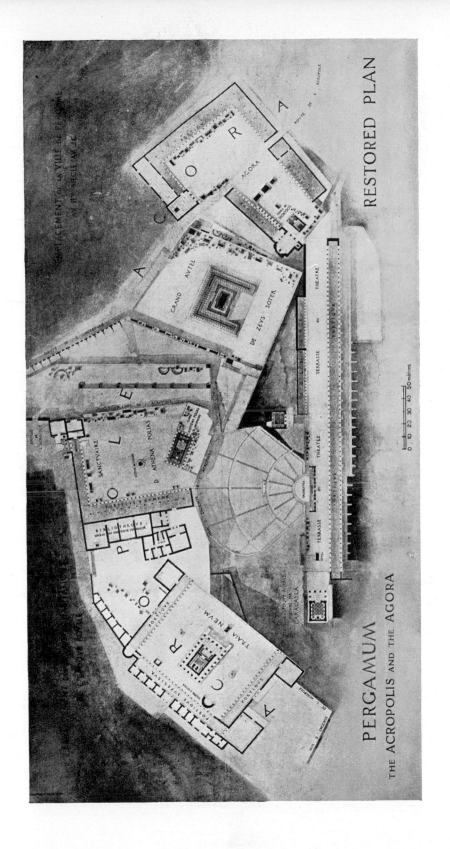

EMPLACEMENT DE LA VILLE DE PERGAME AU III SIÈCLE AV. J.C.

AGORA

RESTORED PLAN

GRAND AUTEL DE ZEVS SOTER

THEATRE

TERRASSE DU THÉÂTRE

PORTIQUE

SANCTVAIRE D'ATHENA POLIAS

BIBLIOTHÈQVE

T. AIA NEVM

PERGAMUM
THE ACROPOLIS AND THE AGORA

0 10 20 30 40 50 mètres

[*a*] Restoration of the Great Altar of *Pergamum*. (See p. 148 above.) In *Berlin*. (viii, 686, 705.)

[*Pergamon, Vol. of Plates III*, Pl. XIV]

[*b*], [*c*] The *horologion* of Andronicus Cyrrhestes, the so-called 'Tower of the Winds,' in *Athens*. Elevation and plan. (viii, 702.)

[Stewart and Revett, *Antiquities of Attica*, I, ch. 3, Pls. II, III]

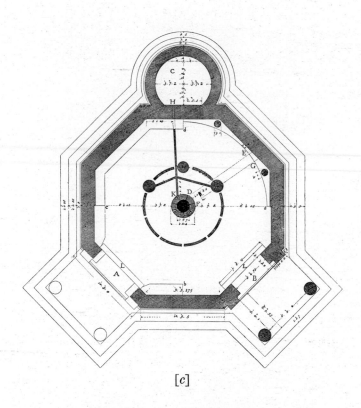

[*c*]

[a] PERGAMUM

[b] THE HOROLOGION

[*a*] A lamp-lighter, cloaked and hooded, carrying a lantern in his right and a ladder in his left hand. Lamp-lighters in the temples of Serapis are mentioned in the papyri. From *Alexandria*; in the *Bibliothèque Nationale, Paris*.

[*b*] A pedagogue carrying the bag of knucklebones for his charge.

[*c*] A gentleman wearing a *chlamys*, perhaps a young Greek delivering his first public address. The cloak is, however, rather long for a *chlamys* and may be intended for a toga, in which case a Roman would be represented.

[*d*] A boy in slave-garb, perhaps a herald, or 'Town-Crier.'

[*b*]–[*d*] In the *Louvre*. (viii, 656.)

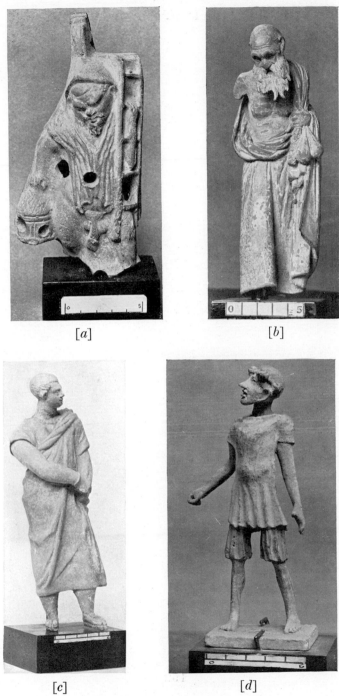

[a] [b]

[c] [d]

TERRACOTTA FIGURINES

[a] An old actor.

[b] A fisherman.

[c] A nurse and child.

[d] A school-girl.

All in the *Louvre*. (viii, 656.)

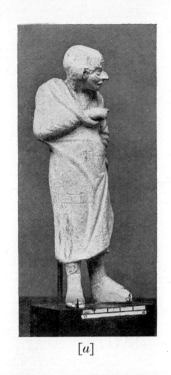

[a]

[b]

[c]

[d]

TERRACOTTA FIGURINES

[a], [b] Terracotta masks from *Carthage*, perhaps apotropaic; but, though caricatures, probably representing typical Carthaginian features.

[*Catal. du Musée Alaoui*, Pls. 72, 1; 74, 5]

[a]

[b]

MASKS FROM CARTHAGE

[*a*] Large votive stele from *Carthage* of Greek style; the architectural decoration, as well as the figure representing Tanit (or Kore), is in the Greek manner. The animal in the pediment is, however, Carthaginian in style.

[*Corpus Inscriptionum Semit.* I, Pl. 41]

[*b*] Terracotta figure of Tanit, the great Punic goddess, found at *Carthage.* While head-dress and fan suggest Egyptian influence, the figure seems purely Carthaginian. Third century B.C. *Bardo Museum, Tunis.*

[*Catal. du Musée Alaoui*, Pl. 76, 1]

[a]   [b]

REPRESENTATIONS OF TANIT

Graeco-oriental figure in painted marble from *Carthage*. This figure forms the lid of a sarcophagus and represents a priestess of Tanit in ceremonial Egyptian garb with wings folded over the skirt. She holds the implements of sacrifice. The Greek element predominates. Fourth to third century B.C. In the *Musée St Louis, Carthage*.

[M. Rostovtzeff, *A History of the Ancient World*, II, Pl. XIV, 2]

A PRIESTESS OF TANIT

CAMBRIDGE: PRINTED BY
W. LEWIS, M.A.
AT THE UNIVERSITY PRESS